UNSUNG HERO

Private Pedro Cano
WW II Medal of Honor Recipient

1946 distinguished service cross ceremony: Gen. Wainwright pins medal on
Private Pedro Cano.

Stephen P. Cano

Contents

Introduction v
The War Begins for Pedro 1
D-Day 2
D-Day Plus 1 4
Northern France Campaign 5
Entering Germany—Attacking the Siegried Line 5
The Hurtgen Forest 5
November 1–9, 1944 Approaching the Hurtgen Forest 7
Hurtgen Forest Battle Launching Point in Zweifall, Germany 9
Entering the Hurtgen Forest 12
Pedro's Company C Attack Plan in Hurtgen Forest 17
Pedro's Company C Attacks, 19 November, 1944 18
The Situation of Pedro's Company C 20, November, 1944 29
Pedro's Company C Situation, 21 November, 1944 33
November 22–December 1, 1944, Hurtgen Forest Battle 36
Heroes 44
December 4–10, 1944, Hurtgen Forest Battle 48
Pedro's 8th Infantry Regiment Departs Hurtgen Forest to Luxembourg 54
The War Ends for Pedro Cano 57
Pedro Cano Receives Distinguished Service Cross in the Mail 57
War Dept. Investigates Army Blunder 63
General Wainwright Agrees to Distinguished Service Cross Ceremony 64
Cano Day Schedule, April 25, 1946 65
Proclamation 66
Wainwright Pins Distinguished Service Cross on Pedro Cano 67
Pedro Cano Killed in Accident 73
Pedro Cano Buried with Military Honors 73
Texas Legislative Medal of Honor 73
2002 Defense Authorization Act 78
President Obama Calls Pedro Cano Family 79
A Letter to President Obama 80
Medal of Honor Ceremony, March 18, 2014 82
U.S. Army Reception 86
Medal of Honor Hall of Heroes Induction Ceremony 87
The Army Song 89
Pedro Cano Army Facts 90
Return to the Hurtgen Forest 90
Endnotes 92

for Pedro

Private Pedro Cano.

Introduction

The first time I heard about Pedro Cano's heroic actions in WWII was when my father, Alvaro Cano, recounted some stories he heard as a young man in Texas. My father was Pedro's first cousin. Although I always listened to my father's stories, I never fully grasped the significance of Pedro's heroic acts on the battlefields of Germany. In time, I came to know Pedro's story in much greater detail and eventually became deeply inspired to preserve Pedro's story for future generations.

This book is my humble attempt to chronicle the journey of WWII Medal of Honor recipient Private Pedro Cano. He was an army soldier in the 4th Infantry Division, 8th Infantry Regiment, 1st Battalion, Company C. Pedro experienced some of the most historical and ferocious battles in American history. His story is one of sacrifice, heroism, historic insult, humility, honor and truth. Pedro survived the war but would come home a "changed" man. But, this is not where his story begins.

At two months of age, Pedro was brought to the United States of America by his parents, Secundino and Nicolasa Cano. He was born in La Morita, Nuevo Leon, Mexico, but raised for virtually his entire life in Edinburg, Texas. He lost his father at a very young age. As a young man, he would often help out others in his neighborhood, fixing radios or doing other odd jobs to help out. He worked hard as a farm worker and was known as a gentle and quiet person. Life was not easy, but Pedro was finding his way. He met Herminia Garza and would marry her. His first child, Dominga, was born in 1943. Pedro was growing a family and establishing deep roots in Edinburg, Texas. Then everything changed in the blink of an eye. On December 7, 1941, the United States was attacked by the Empire of Japan. This attack was the start of WWII and for Pedro, this event was to alter his life forever.

The War Begins for Pedro

Pedro enlisted in the U.S. Army on November 28, 1942. He entered military service on April 28, 1943. His training was based in Fort Meade, Maryland. Pedro was assigned to the 4th Infantry Division which consisted of the 8th Infantry, 12th Infantry and 22nd Infantry. On January 18, 1944, as a member of the 4th Infantry Division, Pedro left from New York Harbor for overseas duty and training. His destination was England, where he would continue his training. In February 1944, it was decided to postpone the invasion of Europe until May 31, 1944. This delay was caused by an increase in the landing forces and an enlargement of the landing areas. The weather, coupled to tidal and light conditions, further deferred the landing date to the first week of June 1944.

Pedro Cano, Ft. Meade, Maryland.

D-Day

Pedro Cano, Ft. Meade, Maryland.

D-Day, June 6, 1944. Pedro's 8th Infantry Regiment took part in the initial assault on Utah Beach on June 6, 1944 starting at H-Hour, or 6:30 A.M. Company C (Pedro's company) was commanded by Captain Robert Crisson, "The spirit and morale of the men were fine. Even after passing what I took to be a naval patrol boat turned upside down, the men continued joking and kidding each other. They had to be reminded not to expose themselves. When we left the boats we had at least 100 yards of water to wade through. Many of the men yelled like Indians when we hit the water, and in fact several had their hair cut similar to Mohawk's (with) a tuft on top of the head."[1] Crisson continued, "The craft landed us and we began working our way down the sand dunes looking for Mud Fort. An NCO reported to me, 'Dammit captain, there's no Mud Fort down here.'[2] The actual leading wave touched the shore 2000 yards south of the planned areas. This point of the beach proved to be lightly defended as compared

D-Day, 8th Infantry Regiment.

D-Day, 8th Infantry Regiment.

to the original beach. All officers agreed that there was only one sensible course of action: move directly inland from their current locations.

Pedro's 1st Battalion was led by Lt. Col. Conrad Simmons. Simmons had the difficult task of striking enemy strong points and then forcing open a causeway over which they had to advance inland toward the 82nd paratroopers. C Company Capt. Robert Crisson recounted, "We moved inland and began to knock out the houses along the road back of the dunes. Company B took Fort Madeleine (about 600 yards inland), assisted by a section of Company C. The left section of Company C took fort U-5 (the coastal strongpoint at La Grande Dune). There was almost no opposition at these forts. Some small arms fire was received from houses along the road, but the Germans gave up gladly when we closed in. A private ran up to me and said, 'I've got two women over here.' I asked him where he had them and he said, 'In a ditch.' I asked: 'What the hell are you doing with two women in a ditch?' He said, 'I don't want them to get shot.' A sergeant chimed in with, 'How old are they?' We immediately moved the two women and a male civilian into a safer spot. We established the Company CP in the church at 444969 (a map coordinate and the site of the tiny Madeleine Chapel, which still stands)."[3]

It was a day of heroic acts. One such act was by Captain Frederick C. Maisel, Jr. of Company I, 8th Infantry Regiment. Captain Maisel led his company across the beach under heavy enemy artillery fire. He proceeded on his assigned mission, meeting strong enemy opposition from strong-points at Germain. The hamlet in Germain was home to some dwellings and a farm. It was defended by a battery of 88mm guns. But by the end of the morning on June 6th, the Germans in these homes began to retreat. They gathered all their equipment and the battery elements and loaded them on trailers pulled by horses. When they departed the farm, they were detected by the infantrymen of Company I commanded by Captain Frederick C. Maisel, Jr. (3rd Battalion). Captain Maisel mounted an ambush and ordered his section chiefs to deploy in the field to the north of the farmhouse. Camouflaged by the presence of an imposing hedge, they were hidden from the Germans. Captain Maisel personally led the attack and they opened fire catching the Germans off guard. The Germans tried to flee, but the horses were unable to accelerate due to the weight of the trailers. A total of 50 Germans and three 88mm guns were captured. This action earned Captain Maisel the Silver Star.

The leading regiment, Pedro's 8th Infantry, moved inland across the three southern causeways and advanced to contact the 82nd airborne forces. The close of D-Day saw their positions in fairly good shape. The 4th Division had its 8th Infantry Regiment east and south of Saint–Mere-Eglise, while the 12th and 22th Regiments were to the northeast between Sainte–Mere–Eglise.[4]

D-Day Plus 1

The morning of D plus 1 saw the elements of the 8th Infantry Regiment launch an attack on the enemy point to the south of STE MERE-EGLISE, with the objective of making contact with the 82nd Division. It had no sooner contacted the 505th in the town when the enemy to the north launched an attack. A coordinated counterattack was planned by both units and by the end of the day, the enemy was cleared from its position. By the night of D plus 1, the VII Corps had a beachhead some 12,000 yards deep and the initial assault had succeeded.[5]

4

Northern France Campaign

The 4th Division would continue pursuing the Germans over the next several months. On June 25, 1944, the Division took part in the capture of Cherbourg on the Cotentin Peninsula. And on July 6–12, 1944, the Division fought near Periers and broke through the left flank of the German Seventh Army, stemming the German drive forward toward Avranches. In August 1944, the Division moved to Paris and assisted the French in the liberation of their capital. Pedro would participate in the famous 4th Division march down the Avenue des Champs d'Elysees in the victory parade.

Entering Germany—Attacking the Siegried Line

On September 14, 1944, the 4th Division attacked the Siegfried Line at Schnee Eifel after moving into Belgium through Houffalize. Pedro was shot in the foot by a German sniper and healed his wound in England before rejoining his company a short time later. Pedro marched with his 8th Infantry Regiment into the Hurtgen Forest battle.

The Hurtgen Forest

On November 6, 1944, the 4th Division would reach the Hurtgen Forest, where a lengthy battle would take place, that lasted until early December. In its one month of fighting in the Hurtgen Forest, the 4th Infantry Division suffered 4,053 battle casualties and more than 2,000 non-battle casualties. Brave men fought side by side. Many died on the battlefield and many would come home forever changed. Four Ivy 4th Division Soldiers received the Medal of Honor for their actions above and beyond the call of duty during the Battle of the Hurtgen Forest—Lt. Col. George Mabry, Jr.; 1st Lt. Bernard Ray; and Pfc. Marcario Garcia and Private Pedro Cano. To all the men who served, this is their story. This is Pedro's story.

Following is the 8th Infantry Regiment and Pedro's Company C daily war journal from November 1, 1994 to December 20, 1944. Also included are some stories from Company C veterans who fought side by side with Pedro Cano.

The Hurtgen Forest covers an area of approximately fifty square miles. It is roughly in the shape of a triangle formed by the three towns of Aachen, Monschau and Duren, Germany. The forest consists of alternative groves of

Hurtgen Forest.

hardwood, large pine and small pine trees. The entire forest is divided into numerous small squares or rectangles with firebreaks approximately forty feet wide separating each square or rectangle. In the most dense portions of the forest visibility is sometimes reduced to as little as ten yards. During the fall of 1944, this area was hit by alternating rain and snow storms. As a result, all roads and trails rapidly became quagmires. The ground was completely saturated with water.[6]

The main enemy defenses consisted of well dug in and well camouflaged individual and automatic weapons positions. These had overhead shelters and were connected by communication trenches. The positions overlooked barriers composed of triple concertina barbwire and minefields containing both anti-tank and anti-personnel mines that were placed in front of, in, and behind the barbwire. All of the barriers were protected by high angle fire as well as small arms fire. These positions were distributed in depth throughout the forest.[7]

Even though every effort was made to obtain dry socks as often as possible and to ensure that the feet of each man were rubbed daily in order to restore circulation, these shortages resulted in extreme discomfort and casualties from trench foot.[8]

November 1–9, 1944 Approaching the Hurtgen Forest

On the 1st of November, the 8th Infantry Regiment was opposed by elements of the 7th AF Festung Battalion, the 4th AF Festung Battalion and the 412th Training Battalion. The enemy held a defensive position along the line of bunkers which was comprised the Siegfried Line, and fortified outposts, that delivered harassing small arms and artillery fire upon the 8th Infantry northern sector. Pedro's 1st Battalion remained in Regimental Reserve and company attack training that involved support of tanks and weapons.[9]

On the following day, November 2nd, Pedro's 1st Battalion was shuttled by truck to the front, relieving the 2nd Battalion in its defensive sector at 1415. The enemy remained within their "bunker line", delivering harassing small arms and occasional mortar and artillery fires in the forward area of the Regiment.[10]

On November 3rd, the 1st Battalion and 3rd Battalion sent strong patrols into enemy territory to determine positions of enemy outposts, minefields, and to capture prisoners. German troops in the opposing line harassed 8rd Infantry patrols and front line positions with heavy machine gun fire

Hurtgen Forest.

but caused few casualties. The 1st and 3rd Battalion patrols captured four enemy prisoners who, while being questioned by the 8th Infantry, exhibited extremely low morale and revealed that their comrades within the Siegfried fortifications held little hope for victory. Enemy long range artillery became more active and increasing numbers of robot bombs were sent across the regimental sector toward rear installations. Although the Cannon Company was unable to fire due to restrictions on ammunition, supporting artillery was active.[11]

On the 4th of November, elements of the 7th AF Festung Battalion, 4th AF Festung Battalion and 412th Training Battalion continued to oppose the 8th Infantry from a defensive position in the Siegfried Bunker Line, delivering harassing small arms, mortar and artillery fire throughout the day. The weather continued cold and rainy. The 3rd Battalion on the right and Pedro's 1st Battalion on the left, continued to hold the Regimental Front, sending Patrol's into "No Man's Land" to capture enemy personnel and obtain information of German activities. The 2nd Battalion, remaining in regimental reserve at Hunningen, conducted training exercises in "woods fighting" and the "attack of a river line". Reconnaissance parties were sent to a new area in preparation for a move by the regiment to a new sector.[12]

On the following day, November 5th, the enemy employed harassing fires, delivered upon the 8th Infantry Sector, and sent two strong patrols against their lines, both of which were repulsed. German troops remaining within their Siegfried fortifications seemed content to improve their defensive positions. A billeting party, consisting of fifteen officers and 30 enlisted men from the 8th Infantry and attached units comprising the combat team, left Hunningen at 0745 under the command of Lt. Col. Bates. They reconnoitered an assembly area and made the necessary billeting arrangements prior to the movement of the combat team to another sector. By 1830, complete relief of the 8th Infantry had been affected by elements of the 9th Infantry Division. The 1st (Pedro's) and 3rd Battalions, Anti-Tank and Cannon Companies, were relieved by the 39th and 60th Infantry Regiments. The 8th Infantry then moved into an assembly area at Hunningen, preparing to move to its new sector.[13]

The movement to the new sector was postponed by Division for 24 hours. The 8th Infantry remained in bivouac near Hunningen during the night. At 1345 on November 7th, an advance group consisting of fifty general purpose vehicles crossed the initial point en route to the new area. At 2200, the remainder of the regiment, moving with transportation and eighty 2-1/2 ton Quartermaster trucks, began a night motor march to its new sector. The Regiment continued its movement by motor during the entire night under difficult conditions of rain and muddy roads. During the blackout poor visibility caused 31 vehicles to slide off the road into the ditch. Two overturned, resulting in six casualties. Upon arrival to the new sector, the regiment immediately began the construction of defensive positions with overhead cover and made preparations for the attack towards Duren. No contact was established with the enemy during the initial occupation of this area which was behind a line held by the 47th Infantry Regiment. Plans were made to reconnoiter forward areas opposing the German defense positions to determine a line of departure for the proposed operation.[14]

On the following day, November 9th, the Regiment remained in its current area, continuing preparations for the attack. Battalion Commanders, Company Commanders and platoon leaders reconnoitered the 47th Infantry Regiment's defense line through which the attack was to be made. The weather continued cloudy with intermittent rains. The 8th Infantry, located in the vicinity of Zweifall, Germany, awaited the order for attack, which was postponed by rain and snow. The Regiment remained in its assembly area, enduring snow, light rain and increasing enemy artillery. They attempted to dig in deeper. But, because of continuous rains, slit trenches could not be dug more than a few inches deep before water would seep in. Therefore, construction of overhead log shelters was essential for protection against tree bursts from artillery as well as the elements.[15]

Hurtgen Forest Battle Launching Point in Zweifall, Germany

On November 10th, the 8th Infantry closed into an assembly area near Zweifall, Germany. The mission of the 4th Division was to seize the crossings of the Roer River in the vicinity of Duren and continue the attack to seize Cologne. The mission of the 8th Infantry was to seize the high ground on the Wenaul Forest, part of the Hurtgen Forest. The enemy units in VII Corps zone from west to east were the 29th Panzer Grenadier Regiment, the 3rd Panzer Grenadier Division, the 246th Fusilier Battalion, elements of the 12th and 275th Infantry Divisions, the 47th Volksgrenadier Division, and elements of the 116th Panzer Division.

On November 11th, overcast, rainy weather again delayed the attack. D-Day was postponed for an additional 24 hours, during which time the

Hurtgen Forest.

troops continued preparations for the jump-off. Additional reconnaissance of the proposed regimental sector was made, and the planning and
coordination of each unit's role was further studied and improved. The 2nd
Battalion moved to its forward assembly area and secured itself for the
night. At 11 o'clock, the Cannon Company moved to a forward position
in preparation for Infantry support. Enemy artillery, increasing in activity,
continued to harass 8th Infantry troops. Toward nightfall the weather
improved somewhat promising that the following day might be more
favorable. The roads were still muddy, making transportation of heavy
vehicles and tanks extremely difficult.[16]

For the past six weeks, the enemy in the sector now facing the 8th Infantry
had well-prepared defensive positions. They had reorganized mixed
elements which had been shattered by the American advance across France
and Belgium. Extensive field works had been dug, protected by obstacles consisting of wire, road-blocks and minefields. Perhaps the greatest
elements of the enemy camouflage and protection was the thick pine forest
stretching for miles along the German front. The trees were so closely
spaced, the foliage so dense, that it was difficult to penetrate, affording the
enemy easy concealment. Although there had been no recent identification
of the enemy force opposing on the opposite side of the 8th Infantry Sector,
they believed that the 365th Training and Replacement Battalion and other
elements of the 275th Division were occupying this sector.[17]

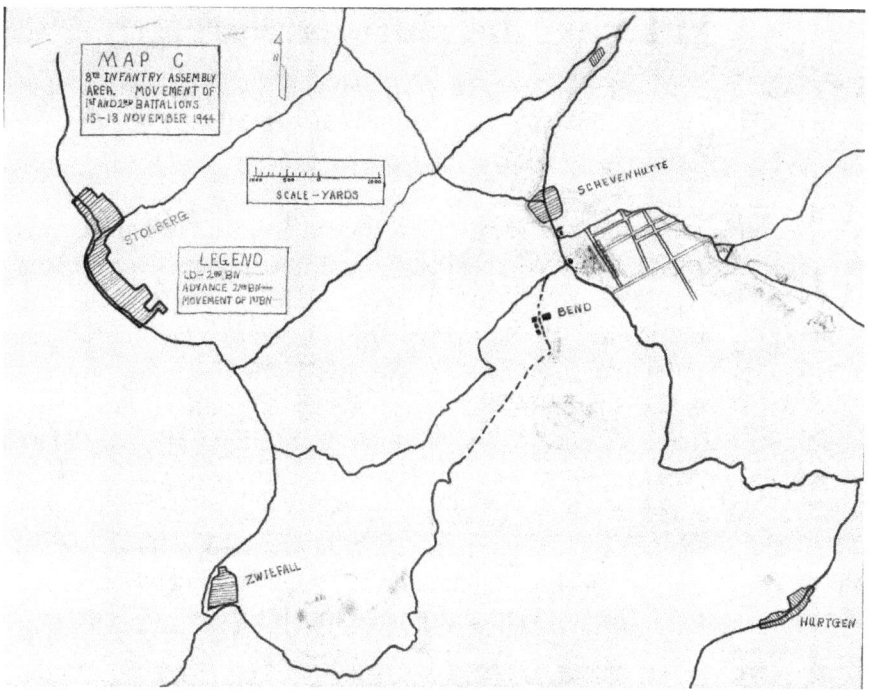

Hurtgen Forest Map, C Company.

This operation was to be one of the largest coordinated attacks that the 4th Infantry Division would participate in since the breakthrough from Normandy on July 25th. The 4th Division was to attack in conjunction with the 1st Infantry Division on the left to seize the crossings of the Roer River near Duren, later pushing northeast to seize Cologne. The 8th Infantry (1st, 2nd and 3rd Battalions) and attached units (Company A, 4th Medical Battalion; one platoon of Company A, 4th Engineer Battalion, two platoons, Company A and D, 70th Tank Battalion, one platoon 803rd Tank Destroyer Battalion and the 29th Field Artillery Battalion in support) were to attack in conjunction with the 26th Infantry Regiment of the 1st Division on its left and with the 22nd Infantry Regiment of the 4th Division on its right. The attack was to be supported by fighter and heavy bombers.[18]

Entering the Hurtgen Forest

"It was a place where it was extremely difficult for a man to stay alive even if all he did was be there. And we were attacking all the time and every day."—Ernest Hemingway, Hurtgen Forest survivor

On November 15th, Pedro's 1st battalion moved from its initial assembly area near Zwiefall to a more advanced assembly area near Bend (see map C).

Early on the morning of November 16th, Division Headquarters sent notice that the Fighter Bombers would attack initial enemy targets at 1115AM. Targets consisted of pill-boxes, field fortifications and lines of supply and reinforcement. H-hour was designated for 1245PM. (Pedro's 1st Battalion remained near Bend until late in the afternoon of November 17th when it moved to the line of departure. Pedro's Company C was about 1200 yards southeast of Schevenhutte. On November 16, 1944 at 1245PM the attack was launched. The 2nd battalion attacked German fortified positions southwest of Duren along with the 26th Infantry Regiment of the 1st

Hurtgen Forest.

Infantry Division. It was the leading assault battalion of the regiment. The attack began after heavy preparation of artillery fire. The battalion crossed the line of departure on schedule and proceeded through a wooded area up a steep hill where a heavy concentration of enemy 150mm artillery fire and 120mm mortar fire fell upon them, inflicting a great number of casualties in Company E and G. The battalion then continued to advance some five hundred yards and finally was held up by three rows of heavy concertina wire protected by machine gun and small arms fire.

Hurtgen Forest.

The 2nd Battalion was once more subjected to heavy artillery and mortar fire, causing even more casualties.[19]

When the Battalion was first attacked by artillery and mortar fire, the company aid men and litter squads of the 2nd Battalion Medical Section immediately aided and assisted the wounded. They alleviated their pain as much as possible with the medical supplies they carried. After treatment by the aid men, the wounded were then carried to the Battalion Aid Station by litter squads for further treatment. These evacuations were carried out during concentrations of heavy artillery and mortar attacks. The shelling occurred as they moved over difficult terrain and down a high hill which was so steep that is was nearly impossible to maneuver litters. The work continued throughout the night and into the morning. The evacuation of the wounded 2nd Battalion soldiers was finally completed on November 17th at 1400. When there was time to count the number of casualties carried in from the field, the total amount was 147, including five members of the medical personnel. After all casualties were evacuated from the field of battle by the medical men of the 2nd Battalion, they were further treated by the medical officers at the Battalion Aid Station. The evacuation to field hospitals was performed through the assistance of ambulance drivers, litter bearers and Company A personnel and the 4th Medical Battalion. They worked throughout the night driving ambulances under the most hazardous road conditions in total darkness. All attempts to breach the concertina wire with bangalore torpedoes failed, so the Regimental Commander ordered the 2nd Battalion to establish a defensive position for the remainder of the day and night.[20]

At 0800 on November 17th, the Regiment continued its advance leading the assault in a column of Battalions against stiffening German resistance. The 2nd Battalion, came upon successive hostile positions of barbed wire entanglements with dug in positions as close as ten yards and as far as 150 yards behind. From these points, the Germans delivered machine gun, mortar and small arms fire upon advancing 2nd Battalion troops, making quick progress impossible. Although repeated attempts were made to breach the concertina wire with bagalore torpedoes, heavy hostile fire made it impossible preventing the 2nd Battalion once again from moving forward.[21]

At 1015 Pedro's 1st Battalion prepared to attack its immediate front or through the 2nd Battalion sector. On November 17th at 1335, the 1st Battalion moved two companies forward to a hill (coordinate 009414) which had been occupied previously by Company F and G. At 1400, with one platoon of tanks, the 1st Battalion, moved along a firebreak toward the 2nd Battalion Sector to break through the enemy concertina wire and advance upon the objective. Simultaneously the 2nd Battalion delivered small arms and mortar fires upon German troops opposing this segment of the line. A short time later, the 2nd Battalion withdrew Companies F and G to an assembly area for reorganization. This was badly needed as a result of the heavy casualties inflicted by the enemy in the bitterly contested advance of the past two days. The 1st Battalion managed to breach one section of concertina wire but was halted by a fierce enemy counterattack driving up a draw (coordinate 020410) at the rear of Company A.[22] At 1510, Pedro's 1st Battalion moved forward advancing to a position parallel to the 2nd Battalion where the 1st and 2nd Battalion lines would be tied in and secured for the night, protecting the right flank of the Regiment. After the counterattack was repulsed by small arms, mortar and artillery fires, the 1st Battalion established a defensive position for the night. Further advances into enemy territory would be impractical because of approaching darkness, bad weather and the character of the enemy defense. The 3rd Battalion had remained in the same position during the entire day and had been prepared to follow the 1st Battalion upon orders.[23] The enemy, dug in at well prepared emplacements behind minefields, road blocks and wire obstacles, delivered increasingly heavy small arms, machine gun, mortar and artillery fire throughout the evening and night. Elements of the 984th Infantry Regiment, 275th Infantry Division and other unidentified units, stubbornly defending their lines, were considered likely to launch a heavy counterattack within 48 hours and only fall back to successive points of defense when pressure against them became overwhelming. In these days of action, Pedro's Company C had lost two officers and sixty three men. The heavy machine gun platoon had lost ten men.[24]

Extensive enemy minefields continued to block routes through the forest. Constant hostile fire made removal of the mines extremely difficult. Trees felled across trails and roads by the enemy impeded troop progress. German fire which made the work of the engineers detailed to remove them very hazardous.

The ground was saturated with water due to rain and snow.[25] Moving forward the 8th Regiment encountered bunkers dug into the ground, automatic weapons positions, individual riflemen and enemy bazookas. Many hand grenades were used and practically all of the fighting was done at ranges under 25 yards. The majority of the trenches and bunkers had been constructed about five yards inside the forest from the edge of the clearing.

Hurtgen Forest.

The bunkers had been constructed so that they extended about three feet above and below the ground. The sides were made of only single large logs, but the roofs were built from three alternating layers of large logs and dirt. Some of the bunkers measured as much as forty feet long and fifteen feet wide. All had beds made of laced rope and straw mattresses.

The forest thickened immediately behind the trenches and bunkers. The large pine trees were so close together that it was impossible for tanks to move any further in that direction. The night was intensely cold, and even though it had not rained during the day, the soil was so wet that the men's uniform were soaked from crawling on the ground. No bedrolls were available since none had been carried. Perhaps the greatest discomfort was caused by wet, cold combat boots. Although each man carried an extra pair of socks there was no way of drying the pair taken off. All personnel were rotated so that each man spent part of the night in the bunkers.

On the following day, November 18th, elements of the 984th German Infantry Regiment and 156th Panzer Grenadier Regiment withdrew slowly to the northwest to prepared positions. They used mortar, artillery and anti-personnel mines to cover the withdrawal.[26] Pedro's 1st Battalion relieved the

2nd Battalion. This relief was not completed until late afternoon. The 1st Battalion was disposed of Companies A and B on line and Company C in reserve.[27]

The Regiment continued the attack in column of Battalions in the order of the 1st, 3rd, and 2nd Battalion. The leading elements of Pedro's 1st Battalion advanced to a location with heavy concentration of concertina wire, covered by artillery mortar and

Pedro Cano, Hurtgen Forest.

small arms fire. There they were held up until tanks that would break the wire were brought forward. One tank succeeded in breaching the wire, forged through and was followed by a column of infantry. About 75 yards to the right of this column, another tank, attempting to breach the wire encountered a minefield and was knocked out. In order to remove the mines from the path of the tanks, the 1st and 3rd squads of the mines platoon and the Anti-Tank Company, were sent forward. Under extremely heavy artillery, mortar and small arms fire, the two squads swept a path approximately 400 yards in length, removing many mines. This enabled the entire battalion to continue the advance. 1st Battalion infantrymen deployed and continued to advance under cover of tank fire until a short time later, when the tactical situation made it advisable to halt for the night and tie in with Company B which had come up from the rear. During the day the 3rd Battalion had prepared to shift two companies forward to support the 1st Battalion operation on call. The 2nd Battalion had continued to reorganize.[28]

Pedro's Company C Attack Plan in Hurtgen Forest

By the morning of November 19th, the exact location of the enemy front lines was still not clearly defined. The Germans had shuffled their forces, concentrating them at strategic points to improve their defense. The enemy's defense line consisted of two man fox holes with overhead cover and well cleared fields of fire, protected by concertina wire on all routes of approach.[29]

The 1st Battalion was to lead the attack. They were ordered to continue the attack at 0900 hours to seize a road junction about 1500 yards to the northeast. Pedro's C Company would commence its forward movement at 0940. The left flank of the Battalion was generally positioned along the Schevenhutte-Duren road and the extension thereof. The right flank of the Battalion was about 1400 yards to the southeast of the Schevenhutte-

Schevenhutte, Germany.

Duren road. The battalions' plan of attack was to attack in the early morning in order of the 1st, 3rd and 2nd battalions. The leading elements of the 1st Battalion would also attack in a column of Companies in the order of C, A, and B. Pedro's Company C attempted to breach the barrier directly to their front. If this attempt was successful, Companies A and B would move in column behind Company C. No close support artillery or 81mm mortar fire would be available since there was great danger of rounds falling short due to the trees. If company C succeeded in breaching the initial minefield then the 1st Battalion would be responsible for further widening and marking the breach. Company C was assigned the mission of attacking astride the firebreak on its left front to breach the barrier that had stopped the 2nd Battalion; cut the Schevenhutte-Duren road; turn to the right astride that road; and capture the Battalion objective. Upon questioning the Battalion Staff, the Company C Commander was informed that no aerial photographs were available for this operation even though there had just been two days of good flying weather.[30]

Pedro's Company C Attacks, 19 November, 1944

Following the completion of the 2nd Battalion relief, the front line 1st Battalion Companies A and B were near the top of a hill about 1,000yards southeast of Schevenhutte, Germany. This hill rises abruptly from the floor of the valley to a height of about 240 feet. Company C, the reserve company, was in position near two rock quarries about halfway up this hill and about 200 yards behind Companies A and B.

Company C was at nearly full strength capacity with 5 officers and approximately 165 men present for duty. The morale and combat effectiveness of the company was at a high peak.

The ground in front of Company C rose steeply for about 200 yards. It then leveled off in the direction of the advance until about 250 yards in front of the final company's objective where a gentle slope extended in to the top of a small hill on which the objective was located. This entire distance, except for the firebreaks, was covered by alternate growths of large pines, small pines and hardwood trees. Immediately in rear of the company the ground sloped sharply down to the floor of a small valley. One narrow road wound up this hill to the rock quarries where Company C was located and thence to the top of the hill where the line of departure was. One tank had

Schevenhutte, Germany.

been able to get up this trail. No other road existed in Company C's zone of attack until the Schevenhutte-Duren was reached. Due to the lack of roads the only route of advance for vehicles was the firebreaks. The ground continued to be saturated with water from the rain and snow.[31]

The tank destroyer platoon near the line of departure would, at H-5 minutes, fire high explosive rounds at the base of the triple concertina wire. This fire would continue until H hour because previously a tank had been unable to break this wire. They had hoped that shell fragments would cut some of the wire making it possible for a tank to go through. But, while attempting to breach this wire with Bangalore torpedoes, the 2nd battalion lost a large number of men to anti-personnel mines. Beginning at H hour the tank destroyers would place automatic fire on enemy positions on both sides of the point where it was planned to breach the barrier. This fire would continue until the bulk of the company passed the barriers.[32]

At H hour one medium tank was to move out and attempt to breach the barrier. If this attempt was successful then the remainder of the medium tank platoon would follow. Then all would move in column straight down

19

Hurtgen Forest.

the left side of the fire-break. If the barrier could not be broken by tanks, then the medium tanks would assist the tank destroyers in protecting the engineer squad while they breached the wire with demolitions.[33]

The platoon of light tanks was to follow the medium tanks through the wire and then immediately turn to the right and move down the right side of the firebreak. Because of the trees, no close support mortar or artillery fire would be available. Beginning at H hour, the mortar platoon of Company D and the 29th Field Artillery would fire on the firebreaks accomplishing company objectives. This intermittent fire would be lifted on call.[34]

Companies A and B along with one heavy machine gun platoon would initially support the attack by fire from their present positions. The line of departure would be the line presently held by Companies A and B. The direction of attack would be astride the firebreak leading to the northeast until the Schevenhutte-Duren road was reached. The direction of attack would then swing to the right and continue astride this road. When the tanks arrived at the rock quarries, they would be supplied with extra ammunition of all types, water and C rations. Pedro's 1st battalion would be responsible for widening and marking the breach in the minefield.[35]

At 0900, the tank destroyer platoon started firing high explosive rounds at the base of the triple concertina wire. They also placed automatic fire on enemy positions. The fire continued until the bulk of Company C passed the barriers. The leading medium tank started forward. At this time, the tank destroyers shifted to firing machine guns at the flanks of the point where the breach was to be made. Company A and Company B and the heavy machine gun platoon began firing as scheduled. As the tank reached the edge of the minefield the explosion of anti-personnel mines could be heard under its tracks. All were nearly breathless as it reached the wire barrier and nosed into it. The tank was momentarily stopped. With a great roar of motors it backed up and charged the barrier again making it through. It was through! Just then one of its tracks was blown off by the explosion of an anti-tank mine.[36]

During this time only occasional mortar and artillery fire had been falling on the barrier. It was later learned from prisoners that when the assembled armor had arrived the enemy had withdrawn and for some reason had failed to shoot concentrations of artillery and mortars on the position. The lead tank had passed through the wire and the attack continued as planned. The next tank in column bypassed the knocked out tank and then cut to the left to position itself on the left side of the firebreak. The passage of the barrier proceeded as planned. Progression of the medium tanks was slowed in order to let the light tanks come abreast. When this was accomplished, the attack proceeded as rapidly as possible. The attack had moved forward about 300 yards when three things happened almost simultaneously:

1) A call was received from the Company Executive Officer stating that the entire Company C had cleared the barrier without the loss of a single man.

2) The leading medium tank was knocked out by a land mine. Fortunately, there were no casualties within the tank or outside it. In fact, the tankers seemed quite happy as they came out of the tank.

3) A concentration of artillery fell on the column.

The column halted because the tanks halted. The medium tank platoon leader was contacted by radio and ordered to continue the advance. The next medium tank pulled around the knocked out tank and the infantry which had been following the lead tank fell in behind it. The occasional pop of anti-personnel mine under the tank could still be heard so the original formation was maintained.[37]

The advance continued about 200 yards farther when the first firebreak running perpendicular to the line of advance was sighted. The Company Commander attempted to contact the medium tank platoon leader by radio, but could not do so. He then attempted to use the telephone on the outside of the platoon leader's tank, but it too was out of order. Contact was only established by him climbing on the tank and getting the turret open. Contact by wire or radio was never reestablished throughout the operation, making adequate control of the tanks very difficult. The column finally halted just short of the firebreak. The engineer squad was called forward and ordered to sweep it. Under the protection of riflemen and tanks, they reported there were no mines on the road.[38]

A patrol consisting of one squad from each column was then ordered to precede the column at the limit of visibility. Flank security was also sent out. This was the first time the Company C Commander felt he could take these actions without excessive loss from mines. The column then started its advance again. Contrary to the reports of the engineer squad, the firebreak did have anti-tank mines in it as seen by the loss of the lead medium tank. The Engineer Squad Leader said it had been a plastic mine and the sweeper would not pick it up. A passage across the road was then probed and the advance continued.[39]

Just after the firebreak was crossed, a firefight involving the two lead patrols broke out and concentrations of mortars and artillery fire began falling on the column. The column was halted and the Company Commander and the 1st Platoon Leader moved forward to assess the situation. They found the two patrols firing on three well camouflaged positions. The lead medium tank and the lead light tank were moved forward and the two patrols and tanks together advanced on the positions. The positions were overrun. Two Germans were captured and three were found dead. The remainder had been able to withdraw due to the excellent selection of their positions and the restricted visibility.[40]

The advance continued and the second firebreak which ran perpendicular to the route was crossed without incident. The majority of the column had crossed this firebreak when the patrols reported they were about 50 yards from the main road that constituted the initial objective of Pedro's Company C and that tanks could not cross the road. A small stream that ran close and parallel to the near side of the road and the abrupt rise of the ground from the stream to the road prevented passage. The presence of this stream had previously been unknown. The patrol further reported that an abatis covered the road for more than a hundred feet and that seven or eight German soldiers had been seen. This information was verified.[41]

Communication wire had not been able to keep up with the advance, but constant contact had been maintained with Battalion CP by radio. The Battalion Commander was informed of the situation and permission granted to change the route of advance and proceed directly to the final objective. It was approximately 1100 hours. The advance had covered about 1,000 yards. There was about 1,000 yards left to go. So far only seven men had been lost to artillery fire. No casualties from small arms fire had been suffered. The change in direction which amounted to a ninety degree turn to the right, was made and the advance continued.[42]

After proceeding for about 300 yards the patrols reported they had arrived at the edge of a space in the woods that had obviously been recently cleared. The column was halted and the Company Commander and the 1st Platoon Leader moved forward to join the patrols. Upon arriving at the edge of the clearing, they found it to be almost a perfect square. It extended for about 250 yards on each side. The felled trees had been removed and, as they later learned, had been used in fortifications. The limbs that had been trimmed from the trees were left in the clearing. Although this square was only approximately 250 yards across, no evidence of fortifications on the far side could be seen even though field glasses were used in searching the area.[43]

The Company Commander felt strongly that this must be a heavily defended area. He decided to make preparations to launch a major attack, even though as yet no enemy had been seen. Accordingly he ordered one patrol to reconnoiter the right flank of the position and the other patrol to reconnoiter the left flank. All platoon leaders and the Field Artillery and Mortar Observers were brought forward and shown the area. Both patrols returned and reported finding an extensive trench system on each flank of the position. This confirmed the Company Commander's suspicion that this was a strongly fortified position. He determined to throw everything in the first assault in an attempt to avoid being repulsed.[44]

The platoon leaders were withdrawn, and the attack order was issued. The order given was as follows:

(1) The 1st Platoon, Company C, would move to the left flank and attack both sides of the trenches.

(2) The 2nd Platoon, Company C, would swing around to the right in order to position itself parallel to the trench system, which made up the far side of the clearing. It would then attack astride those trenches and join with the 1st Platoon at the far left corner of the square.

(3) The 3rd Platoon, Company C, would move down the right side of the square to protect the flank of Company C and be prepared to assist the 2nd Platoon.

(4) The attached heavy machine gun platoon from positions in the 1st Platoon area would support the attack of the 1st Platoon and be prepared to support the attack of the 2nd platoon. It would fire until:

(a) its fires were masked by the 1st Platoon;

(b) ordered to stop by the Company C Commander;

(c) the red star signal from the 2nd platoon.

This platoon's fire was not expected to be very effective since it could not secure positions at the very edge of the clearing. The forest was so thick that from positions just a few feet inside it the field of fire was very limited.

(5) The platoon of tank destroyers and the remaining two medium tanks would move into position, where they could fire directly across the clearing. All of the weapons on the tanks would be fired. This fire would be lifted under the same conditions as stated for the heavy machine gun platoon.

(6) The light tanks would move directly across the clearing until they arrived at the far edge, where they would continue firing into the woods. This fire would be lifted under the same conditions as the fire of the heavy machine gun platoon. The light tanks needed to advance because so little was known about the clearing, that it was felt they might be needed beyond it. The forest on the far side of the clearing looked too dense for medium tanks to advance.

(7) The light machine guns of the Weapons Platoon would remain with the platoons they were presently attached to.

(8) The 60mm mortar section was to go into position at the last fire-break and fire on the far edge of the clearing.

(9) The fire of all supporting weapons would begin three minutes prior to the jump-off and would continue under the conditions imposed, except for the 60 mm mortar section which would cease firing at the end of the three minutes.

(10) The artillery and mortar observers would call for protection fire to support the battalion objective since close support could not be provided to support the attack.

(11) The engineer squad would remain in the immediate vicinity of the medium tanks.

(12) The Company Executive Officer would carry a SCR 300 radio, and remain with the platoon leader of the medium tank platoon. In this manner, radio communication could be constantly maintained between the tank platoon leader and the company commander.

(13) All artillery fires were to begin on the order of the Company C Commander, and the attack was to proceed as planned thereafter.[45]

So far, all plans and preparations had been made more on the "hunch" of the Company C Commanding Officer than on any concrete intelligence concerning the enemy. At approximately 1230 hours, all units were moved into position. The Company C Commander stood up to make final check and picked up the hand set of the radio to inform the Battalion Commander that the attack was about to be launched. Suddenly, the air became saturated with small arms and high angle fire. Rifle fire, machine gun fire, artillery up to 170 mm and mortar fire ranging from 60 mm to 150 mm rained upon Company C. This veteran company had never experienced such sudden and overwhelming fire. The impeccable timing of the German attack was unbelievable. The company commander's radio operator was severely wounded and the radio destroyed by small arms fire. The 2nd Platoon Leader and the Weapons Platoon Leader were also badly wounded. The number of other wounded personnel is unknown. There was no cover from this rain of death. The enemy mortar and artillery shells striking and exploding in the tree tops were particularly effective. Due to air bursts, no man could find shelter from the shell fragments. The company was completely disorganized during this time.[46]

The Company C Commander immediately decided the only option was attack as soon as control was regained. The Executive Officer was ordered to take command of the 2nd Platoon. But, it was soon evident that he had been too badly shaken by the German attack to do so. He was then relieved of this duty and ordered to supervise the evacuation of the wounded and ensure that no man evaded combat by leaving the area. The platoon sergeants of the 2nd Platoon and Weapons Platoon were ordered to assume command of those platoons. A SCR 300 radio was obtained from the Weapons Platoon and contact was reestablished with the Battalion's C.P. The reorganization required took approximately a half hour. It was extremely difficult to reorganize due to the constant and intense concentration of high angle and small arms fire that blanketed the area.[47]

Just before the attack resumed, a P-47 started strafing what first appeared to be the area occupied by the 1st Platoon, Pedro's Company C. However, the P-47 was actually strafing the opposite side of the clearing, only 250 yards in front of Company C.[48]

The three minute attack preparation was ordered. Then the P-47 made another attack, and then just as the preparation ended, the P-47 made its last attack. No prior planning could have coordinated such perfect support from the Air Corps. The order to attack was given. The 2nd platoon had not advanced more than fifty yards, when the platoon leader reported they were encountering bunkers dug into the ground, automatic weapons positions and individual riflemen. He was ordered to press the attack and pass through the bunkers leaving only one or two men to guard each until the 3rd Platoon could arrive to clean them out. The 1st Platoon reported encountering well dug-in positions, but that those were being slowly overcome. The platoon of light tanks had moved out and advanced slowly across the clearing. Enemy bazookas started firing but were extremely inaccurate. With such heavy fire being placed on enemy positions, gunners probably could not accurately aim their weapons. The Company Commander then moved forward with the 3rd Platoon. The 1st Sergeant was ordered to remain with the tank platoon leader instead of the Executive Officer, who was busy with the last duties assigned him. The lack of direct communication with the tank platoon leader was once more proving to be problematic. The 3rd Platoon arrived in rear of the 2nd Platoon and started clearing out the bunkers. The light tanks were stopped about fifty yards short of the edge of the clearing, by a maze of barbed wire attached to short stakes. Since they were more or less "sitting ducks" in that position, they were ordered to return across the clearing. All infantry elements of the company moved forward slowly. Fierce fighting took place in each platoon area. Many hand grenades were used and practically all of the fighting was done at ranges under 25 yards. At last, the 1st Platoon reported it had fought its way to the corner of the square where the 2nd Platoon was to join it. The 1st Platoon was ordered to remain in position, since any further advance would have exposed it to 2nd Platoon fires. Shortly thereafter, the 2nd Platoon advanced sufficiently allowing the tank fire to be lifted. The Heavy Machine Gun Platoon had ceased firing before this. The 2nd Platoon then fought its way to a junction with the 1st Platoon. In the meantime, the 3rd Platoon completed its mopping up mission. The consolidation and reorganization of troops began immediately.[49]

In the attack on the clearing, twenty five Germans were captured and fifteen were killed. Every German captured had been wounded as the enemy had resisted to the utmost. It was now 1630 hours. With the approaching darkness, it was evident that Company C would be unable to advance further that day. The Battalion Commander was informed of the Company C status. A check revealed that in the day's action, Company C had lost two officers and sixty three men; the heavy machine gun platoon lost ten men and the engineer squad lost one man. No personnel were lost in the tank or tank destroyer platoons, despite three medium tanks being knocked out by mines.[50]

All three rifle platoons were placed in line on two sides of the square facing the enemy. The 60 mm mortar section and the armor were ordered to remain in position. The heavy machine gun platoon was brought across the clearing and dispersed in squads along the front occupied by Company C. Upon closer inspection of the position just captured, they found the majority of the trenches and bunkers had been constructed about five yards from the edge of the clearing inside the forest. The bunkers had been constructed so that they extended about three feet above and below the ground. The sides were made of only single large logs, but the roofs consisted of three alternating layers of large logs and dirt. Some of the bunkers measured as much as forty feet long and fifteen feet wide. All contained beds made of laced rope and straw mattresses.[51]

Had aerial photographs of this area been available the battalion would have known this clearing existed, and plans could have been made beforehand for its capture. Time and lives might have been saved.[52]

Immediately behind the trenches and bunkers, the forest was very dense. The large pine trees were so close together that tanks could not move any further in that direction. A small patrol was sent to the front to determine the location of the next German position. Another small patrol was sent to the right to see if tanks could advance in that direction. The first patrol returned and reported the dense pines extended about 100 yards and then gave way to large hardwood trees. This was about 250 yards from the 1st Battalion and Company C objective. As the patrol leader emerged from the pines, he was fired upon by an automatic weapon from the direction of the objective. A short while later, the second patrol returned and reported that the dense forest extended so far to the right that tanks would be unable to advance in that direction. All of this information was given to the Battalion Commander by radio.[53]

All of the water, ammunition and food that had been carried on the tanks were brought forward to the positions presently occupied. The 1st Platoon was ordered to establish one listening post at the edge of the thick pines. Almost immediately after Company C had captured the clearing, high angle fire started falling within the area. This fire was intense while day light lasted, with harassing fire continuing throughout the night.[54]

Companies A and B had followed Company C all day. Although Company A and Company B had not participated in the attack they had suffered severe casualties from heavy small arms fire and mortar, artillery and tank fire. Just before dark, these companies moved forward and joined

Company C. At this time, Company C consolidated its position so that it occupied only the trenches on the side of the square that faced northeast. Company A moved to the left and Company B to the right of Company C to form a perimeter defense of the square.[55]

It was rapidly getting dark and many of the wounded lay where they had been hit. Some were unable to move due to the nature of their wounds, while others were immobile from the shock. The litter carry now involved a one way distance of about 1800 yards, 500 of which was through known or suspected minefields that had only been marked by the tank tracks. As yet this path had not been widened or marked by the Battalion. Litter teams were therefore restricted to following the tank tracks while moving through that area. Mortar and artillery fire were causing litter team casualties. It was soon evident that all the wounded could not be evacuated from the battlefield that night. All companies began searching for the wounded and brought them to the bunkers where they could at least have shelter and receive first aid. This search went on far into the night since the moans of the wounded led the searche's to them. The litter teams continued working throughout the night, but in spite of their tremendous efforts, all of the wounded were not evacuated by morning.[56]

The night was intensely cold. Even though it had not rained during the day, the ground was so wet that the men's clothing was soaked through from crawling. No bedrolls were available since none had been carried. All efforts were being directed towards evacuating the wounded. Perhaps the greatest discomfort was caused by wet cold combat boots. Even though each man carried an extra pair of socks, there was no way of drying the pair taken off. All personnel were rotated so that each man spent part of the night in the bunkers. During this time, he was required to remove his boots and rub his feet to restore circulation. Throughout that day, no other unit in the Regiment attacked the enemy.[57]

The Situation of Pedro's Company C 20, November, 1944

During the night telephone communications with the Battalion CP were established. On November 20th, shortly before daybreak, the Batallion Commander ordered the Company C Commander by telephone to attack again at 0900 hours in the same hour as the previous day. No close support mortar or artillery fire would be available, since there was such a great danger of the rounds striking the tall trees overhead. The objective remained the same as the final objective of the previous day.

Company C's plan of attack was generally as follows:

(1) The 1st and 3rd Platoons would attack abreast, with the 3rd Platoon on the right.

(2) The 2nd Platoon would follow in rear of the 1st Platoon.

(3) The light machine gun section would be attached to the 3rd Platoon.

(4) The heavy machine gun platoon, which in the course of its reorganization had dwindled down to a section, would be attached to the 1st Platoon.

(5) All of the armor would remain in its present location.

(6) The 60mm mortar section would move into the clearing and be prepared to deliver fire on the objective.

(7) Company Headquarters would remain in its present location until ordered to displace.

(8) The engineer squad would remain with the Company Headquarters and be prepared to use demolitions if the company encountered a minefield.

(9) The artillery and mortar observers were ordered to request fire on the roads in rear of the objective.

(10) The direction of the attack would be due east.

(11) The line of departure would be in the trenches now occupied by Company C.[58]

After daybreak, the company reorganization was checked again. Four men had been wounded during the night. This left a total force of 3 officers and 98 men in Company C. The Battalion sent a message that the minefield had finally been cleared and additional litter teams were being deployed. Since daybreak, the enemy artillery and mortar concentrations had steadily increased in intensity. By 0830 hours, seldom did a period of five minutes go by without a concentration falling on the clearing. Evacuation of the wounded or any other movement was incredibly difficult.[59]

At 0900 hours, Pedro's Company C moved out of its trenches. The company had just moved fifty yards when concentrations of mortars, artillery fire and tank fires fell into the trenches. The tree bursts of the high angle fire exacted a heavy toll on the troops. The company pushed steadily forward. Upon arrival at the edge of the thick pines the two leading platoons sent scouts further ahead, deployed more men and then moved into the hardwood forest. Visibility here was as much as 100 yards in some directions.[60]

Shortly after leaving the thick pines, the high angle fire decreased in intensity, since the slight slope of the ground caused the artillery shells to pass on overhead. The company moved 100 yards from the edge of the thick pines. The scouts were only about 50 yards from the objective when, suddenly, the enemy opened fire with machine guns, rifles, bazookas and direct fire weapons. The scouts were all either killed or wounded. Several casualties were sustained in each of the leading platoons. The company was halted. Although several enemy machine guns were firing, only two could be definitely located. Bazookas and rifle grenades were brought forward to fire on these positions. The majority of the rounds fired by the bazookas failed to go off due to landing short and striking soft ground. One machine gun position was silenced. The refile grenades were of little value since a direct hit could not be scored with them.[61]

The two leading platoons were ordered to move forward by fire and movement with all squads abreast. They attempted to advance but did not gain more than a few yards at the cost of several casualties, among which was the Platoon Leader of the 1st Platoon. The company was stopped again. The Executive Officer was called forward to take command of one of the platoons. Just as he joined the Company Commander, a mortar round burst in the tree over them, and the Executive Officer had to be evacuated. The only officer left was the Company C Commander.[62]

The 1st Platoon did not have a platoon sergeant or platoon guide since both had been wounded on the first day. The Platoon Guide of the 3rd Platoon was placed in command of the 1st Platoon. It was impossible to maneuver to the left since a machine gun from an unknown position was sweeping the ground in that area. The 2nd Platoon was ordered into a position on the right flank of the company. When it was in position, the 60 mm mortar section was ordered to fire on the objective even though some rounds might fall short. As soon as the mortar section started firing another attack was launched and again the attack was stopped. Seemingly, the fire of the 60 mm mortar section had no effect, as more casualties were sustained. It was now about 1400 hours. The Battalion Commander had been kept informed of the situation all day and was now informed that Company C had been completely stopped.[63]

Neither Company A nor Company B had moved throughout the day. About 1430 hours Company A was ordered to attack on the left of Company C and Company B was ordered to attack on its right. Company C was ordered to join in the attack. Shortly after Company A moved out of its position, they placed one squad on the high ground across the road on the left flank of the battalion. From this vantage point, they could explain the "supernatural" fire of the enemy. A well dug-in, camouflaged, enemy artillery observation post was captured.[64]

Both Company A and Company B launched their attack, but neither ever got abreast of Company C. Company C was unable to move. Just before dark, Company C withdrew approximately fifty yards to occupy better positions. The men were located far enough down the hill to move around stooped over and able to avoid getting hit by small arms fire. In the most advanced positions, it was impossible to even rise to one's knees without becoming an immediate target of enemy small arms fire.

The results of the day's action were:

(1) Company C had advanced only about 150 yards.

(2) Many casualties had been suffered.

(3) It could not be definitively established that a single enemy combatant had been killed or wounded. None had been captured.[65]

The need for reorganization was immense. The total non-commissioned officer strength remaining in the forward area included the 1st Sergeant, the Weapons Platoon Sergeant, one Platoon Guide, three Rifle Squad Leaders, and one Light Machine Gun Squad Leader. The Light Machine Gun Section consisted of a squad leader and two men. Company Headquarters was reduced to the 1st Sergeant and a radio operator. This did not include the Supply Sergeant and six cooks. The Weapon Platoon Sergeant and six men remained in the 60mm mortar section. Forty men were present in the forward area. It was then decided to temporarily disband the 60 mm mortar section, since they could not find close-in support in this particular area. Two men from this section were assigned to the light machine gun section so that both guns of that section could be manned. The remaining four men became riflemen and consolidated into two platoons. The remaining platoon guide was placed in command of one platoon and the Weapons Platoon Sergeant commanded the other. One platoon had sixteen men and the other had seventeen. The light machine gun section had five men. During the day's fighting, two officers and fifty men became casualties.[66]

The heavy machine gun platoon was reduced to eight men. Its Platoon Leader was returned to the bunkers in the clearing. Any further action on his part would have resulted in another casualty due to combat fatigue. While this reorganization was being made, an order was received directing the detachment of the engineer squad and the armor, requesting return to the CP Battalion immediately. The CP Battalion had moved to a location near the rock quarries. These units left in order to report to the new location at once. All of the wounded were evacuated prior to darkness, but it was not possible to remove the dead. The Supply Sergeant took care of the ammunition shortage and the mess personnel acted as carrying teams during the night.[67]

The company was disposed for the night in a single straight line that extended from a point near the road on the left flank for about 150 yards to the southeast. The two heavy and two light machine guns were spaced equally along this line. Actual contact on the left flank was not made with Company A, but was established on the right flank with Company B. The men started digging holes for the night but soon found that the hole not be more than six inches deep. The hole started filling with water because the ground was water-soaked. The men had learned time and again during the past two days that shelter trenches dug in the woods were practically useless unless they could be covered with logs. Since this could not be done in the given situation, attempts to dig ceased. Bed rolls were still not available, since all efforts had been directed towards evacuating the wounded and resupplying of ammunition. Soon after dark, it became bitterly cold, and, as the clothing was water-soaked, the only way to keep warm was through exercise. This night was spent in alternate periods of exercise and rest. No one was able to sleep. Once more the most severe discomfort was caused by inadequate footwear. The only comfort during the night was that the majority of the enemy artillery rounds were passing overhead and landing in the rear. Only occasional mortar rounds fell on the position during the night. No order was received from Battalion.[68]

Pedro's Company C Situation, 21 November, 1944

On November 21st, all troops anxiously awaited dawn and the little warmth it would bring. In the first false light of the sunrise the Germans launched a counterattack of approximately one platoon strength. Eight Germans were killed and four were captured. The attack was repulsed. Five members of Company C were wounded, including the Platoon Guide acting as Platoon Leader. The total fighting strength of Company C was now one officer and thirty five men. Aside from the 1st Sergeant, only the Weapons Platoon Sergeant remained in the forward area.[69]

This information was relayed to the Battalion Commander, who then ordered Company C to withdraw to the clearing and await for the 3rd Battalion to pass through at 0800 hours. When it did, the fighting from November 19–21 stopped for Pedro's Company C.[70]

The 3rd Battalion advanced against the enemy to destroy all German forces east and west of a road located at coordinate 019402 to 0231393. Company L advanced toward the south meeting small arms fire. Company I took up position in support of Company L. A short time later, this force met a German tank, half-track and infantry troops. After a skirmish, they captured 29 prisoners. Elements of the 3rd Battalion then made contact with the 22nd Infantry Regiment. Having mopped up all enemy resistance in this area, the 3rd battalion pulled back to an assembly area for the night. Meanwhile, intelligence reports indicated that the enemy continued to improve field fortifications along the entire front. They shuffled their troops from one point to another to meet the increasing pressure of the First Army units driving through the line.

Briefly, the results of the operation were: Company C did not gain its objective, but it did make an advance of approximately 1800 yards. In making this advance it created a breach in one very large minefield and captured fiercely defended major position. This strongpoint was the key to the enemy defenses in that particular area of the forest. The total known enemy losses including the dead and captured was 57. Company C and attachments lost a total of 148 men and three medium tanks. These losses were high, but expected, considering the high terrain and how stubbornly defended and well prepared enemy positions were.[71]

For its actions, Company C was commended by Order of the Day, Number 68, 5 January 1945, Headquarters 4th United States Infantry Division.[72]

Many of those wounded on November 19th were not evacuated until November 20th. This resulted in much additional suffering and possibly in death for a few. This failure in prompt medical treatment was due to four things:

(1) The extremely high number of personnel wounded not just in Company C, as well as in the remainder of the Battalion .

(2) The litter carry was long, involving an evacuation route of approximately 1800 yards from the point where the majority of the men were wounded to the Battalion Aid Station.

(3) Since a path through the minefield had not been marked other than by tank tracks, the litter teams were restricted to those tracks and were thereby slowed down.

(4) Even though additional litter teams were deployed a greater number of them should have been secured since all units that had participated in this area had suffered severe casualties.[73]

Company C's plan of action did not include a widening or marking of any breach it was successful in making in the initial minefield. The tank tracks were deemed to be sufficient marking until the Battalion further widened and marked the breach. The Battalion did not carry out this on November 19th. This failure resulted in troops traveling excessive distances. Without knowing the depth of the minefield, they were forced to only follow the path left by the tank tracts as they made their way to or from the rifle companies.[74]

On November 19th the only actual Assault Company in the Regiment was Company C. This allowed the defenders to mass their fires on Company C Had other units been deployed in the attack, there would have probably been less casualties and the troops would have advanced further.[75]

Neither Company A nor Company E was actually committed until about 1430 hours on November 20th. By this time, Company C had lost the majority of its combat efficiency. Had these two units been committed earlier the battalion's objective probably would have been achieved that day.[76]

The attached heavy machine gun platoon did not fire all of the ammunition it had carried. Yet all members of the platoon, with the exception of one squad, became casualties. The platoon fired in the attack on only one occasion, the November 19th attack on the clearing. But, the fire was not effective on either occasion due to their inability to find adequate firing positions. The guns could not be emplaced on the very edge of the clearing, plus a position as much as five yards within the thick forest resulted in very limited fields of fire. It was therefore felt that the support rendered by a heavy machine unit in the attack in woods of this type was not sufficient to justify the high loss of personnel.[77]

Only one radio and one telephone, both on one tank, was provided to control communication of two platoons of tanks and one platoon of tank destroyers. This lack of communications foresight proved to be a great hindrance in rapidly controlling the units. The company more or less stumbled onto the clearing in the forest. Had they known of the clearing's existence, they would have made plans to capture it beforehand, probably dramatically reducing the loss of men and time spent on its capture. No aerial photographs of the area were available. Since the square was cleared only shortly before the attack, it was not mapped. Photographs should have been available.[78]

By far, the majority of losses sustained were due to enemy artillery and mortar fire. This fire was particularly effective because in the majority of cases, the rounds burst upon contact with the trees, thereby creating air bursts. When the company was stopped, the men attempted to dig in. However, they found their digging was of little value, since overhead protection could not be provided.[79]

Private Bill Loy of Company "C" recalled that as they got deeper into the Hurtgen Forest, the supply lines got further behind them. About 6 people would be given the duty to go back at night for supplies, water and food for the next day. Bill Loy was one of the men selected. Many of the chosen men never made it back. They simply disappeared, never to be seen again. They had no idea what happened to them. So the next night they would send six more men and those men disappeared. In the meantime, Bill Loy would be filling up his canteen with muddy water surrounded by dead men. One night, Bill was really hungry and didn't want to drink muddy water. So Bill volunteered to go back for supplies. He told his commander he thought he knew where the food supplies were being dumped. Bill had some experience with night walking. As a boy back home in Elon, North Carolina, Bill often went Possum hunting at night with his dad. He knew how to check for moss on the north side of the trees, watch the stars for guidance and keep the wind in his face because he knew the wind was coming from the north. Several days earlier, his Company "C" had run into a minefield and lost many men. The engineers came in with equipment and identified the mine locations. They ran a rope as a path guide for the soldiers to follow safely through the minefield. So Bill knew if he found that rope he could safely cross the minefield. Luckily, Bill found the rope in the pitch dark and made it safely across the minefield. He found the supply location shortly thereafter. Another volunteer had joined Bill on their supply trip. They couldn't carry enough supplies for the entire company but carried everything they could. They finally arrived back at the company about 2am. All the men were dug in. After their successful supply run, Bill led the small party back for supplies every night. So he would fight all day and then spend most of the night going back for supplies. Bill became exhausted and eventually the other soldiers complained that he was being worked to death. After that, Bill was allowed to only lead the supply run but did not have to carry supplies back. The other men carried the supplies.[80]

November 22–December 1, 1944, Hurtgen Forest Battle

At 0930 on November 22nd, Pedro's 1st Battalion started their attack. The support of 2nd Battalion heavy weapons greatly aided their advance but also brought heavy hostile artillery fire upon 2nd Battalion mortar positions. After having encountered strong enemy resistance, Companies A and B fought their way northeast to their first objective and had captured a number of Germans by 1040. At 1120, the 3rd Battalion moved along the 1st Battalion axis of advance until forced to halt temporarily before increasing enemy resistance. At 1300, Companies I and K engaged the enemy in a heavy fire fight. They fought their way forward and then turned to the southeast killing and capturing a large number of German troops. Pedro's Company C moved to the left of Company B and fought its way through continuous mortar, artillery and small arms fire. Company A finally reached the vicinity of Jager-Haus (F034424).[81]

The 2nd Battalion led the renewal of the Regiment attack at 0840 on November 23rd. For a short time, they made rapid progress taking a large number of prisoners. Difficulties in resupply delayed the advancement of the 3rd Battalion. They did not move forward until 0900, but were only able to advance slowly against intense small arms, machine gun, mortar and artillery fire—all of which pinned down leading elements at several points.

The Cannon Company, meanwhile, fired on enemy targets opposing the infantry advance. Companies K, I and L moved to coordinates 042421, 037420 and 044416, where they assumed a defensive position. The 2nd Battalion continued its progress southeast toward its objective, where Companies E and F tied in with Company G to their immediate rear. Elements of the German 1058th Infantry Regiment and 1057th Infantry Regiment retired to prepared positions before increasing the pressure of the 8th Infantry troops. But later in the day, they launched several counterattacks to regain lost ground. In the northern half of the Regimental Sector, the enemy attacked with an assault platoon of 25 men to regain their main line of resistance. This attack was repulsed. After putting up a stubborn defense and retiring only after being severely mauled, the enemy launched a desperate counterattack to retake their former position in the southern half of the Regimental Sector. Heavy artillery and mortar fire supported these attempts and landed all along this segment of the line. The counterattacks were quickly beaten off and many prisoners were taken. Upon interrogation, prisoners captured in this action said that the morale of the average German soldier from this section of the front was rather low. Extensive allied aerial activity behind the German lines was rapidly weakening the Reich's defensive power. Enemy troops were experiencing shortages in food, clothing and other supplies. Due to heavy enemy fire in Pedro's 1st Battalion sector they had been unable to move during the day. But at 1515, Pedro's Company C was able to move behind Company A and tie in on the left flank of Company I. Company B, heavily hit in previous actions, was pulled back to receive replacements and to rest. Although all areas occupied by the 8th Infantry were under continual hostile mortar and artillery fires, the engineers worked without rest in a desperate effort to build supply lines and roads through the deep woods and over the soggy ground.[82]

Private Bill Loy from Elon, North Carolina and fellow Company C soldier, had some very close calls in the Hurtgen Forest. One night he was digging his foxhole and then his commander decided it was too crowded so he ordered Bill to move to point. Nobody wanted to be point but Bill followed orders and as he departed for the point, an artillery shell came in and landed in the hole he had just left and almost finished digging. Three men had jumped in the hole and were blown up. There was nothing left of them. Bill had to sign a paper confirming the identities of the three men because they could no longer be identified.[83]

On November 24th, the Regiment moved forward in a resumption of the attack at 0830. Pedro's Company C led the 1st Battalion attack, and was able to move forward early. The 2nd Battalion, with Companies E and F abreast, met with extremely heavy machine gun and small arms fire. Nevertheless, they continued advancing slowly and cautiously southeast toward the objective. They captured considerable enemy equipment, weapons and prisoners. The enemy fought a bitter defense employing direct fire weapons against the 3rd Battalion. In the Regimental Northern Sector, the enemy launched a small counterattack to regain lost ground but was immediately driven back. Artillery and mortar interdiction and harassing fires continued to slow down the progress of infantrymen. The numerous mines and road blocks restricted the routes of advance within the entire sector. By the end of the day, the 2nd Battalion had reached its objective (045427). When the 1st Battalion objective was taken, Companies B and C were drawn to the rear and the 3rd Battalion took over the 1st Battalion area, guarding the roads. The engineers continued to work under fire, clearing the main the supply route and the supply routes to battalions. However, work progressed slowly because of the heavy shelling.[84]

Lt. John C. Ausland, a 23 year old in the 29th Field Artillery Unit, told an interesting story. Before they got to the Hurtgen Forest, Lt. Col. Cyril J. Letzelter had replaced Jack Meyer as commander of the 1st Battalion. Meyer had commanded it for a short time in Normandy but was wounded. Although a likeable person, other officers agreed with Ausland that there was something lacking in Letzelter. In the Hurtgen, he would return at night to the Battalion's command post. Ralph Thomas, the Battalion S-3 and Ausland would plan the next day's attack. Thomas would prepare orders for the company commanders and Ausland would prepare the artillery. Early in the morning, Letzelter would return to their forward command post, and the attack would begin. If the companies ran into trouble during the day, their commanders would get together and decide how to deal with it.

One day, an awkward situation arose when the regiment decided to have tanks attack along a road. The tank commander was clearly unenthusiastic about moving through the forest, since the German's had anti-guns and the handheld panzer faust. About the same time as the tank commander showed up, so did Col. Richard G. McKee, who had replaced Col. Rodwell as Commander of the 8th Regiment. The tank commander posed increasingly difficult questions to Letzelter, which he had difficulty answering. Finally, Col. McKee intervened and the tanks set off down the road. A short time, later a commander of one of the tanks showed up sobbing. A German shell had hit their tank and his best friend had had his face blown off.

There was another pause, and the Germans took advantage of it to move reinforcements into the forest opposite them. At this point, however, Col. McKee ordered the 2nd Battalion to make a big demonstration with artillery, smoke, etc. It then remained in place while the 1st Battalion moved forward with no artillery or mortar preparation. This tactic worked well. The Germans fired their artillery and mortars at the demonstrating battalion which remained in covered dugouts. Pedro's 1st Battalion moved forward without resistance until it reached its objective - a monastery in the forest at Gut Schwarzenbroich. But there, it ran into German resistance.[85]

The 2nd Battalion moved forward in attack at 1130 on November 25th, meeting slight small arms and mortar fire. The enemy withdrew in the face of increasing infantry pressure supported by heavy concentrations of artillery. But at 1330 the enemy troops launched a counterattack with approximately fifty men. This attack was quickly repulsed and the Battalion reached its objective (047407) at 1410. Company K and L strengthened their position while Company I sent aggressive patrols to the north. As Company A withdrew, the Fourth Cavalry Squadron took over the defense of the

Hurtgen Forest, 8th Infantry Regiment.

Jager-Haus area and the hill to the northeast of it. Tactical air missions, which had been requested to support the 8th Infantry advance, could not be carried out because of the weather. However, the 29th Field Artillery Battalion was able to maintain a liaison plane in the air to cover the 2nd and 3rd Battalions as they moved anti-tank guns and tank destroyers into position for further operations. Eemy artillery and mortars continued to be active throughout the day. Despite covering the Regimental Sector with a recurrent barrage of high explosives, the combat engineers continued to work against time, pushing supply routes ahead. By the end of the day, the supply route to the 2nd Battalion was completed and being used. Critical supplies were now delivered with greater speed and in greater quantity when needed.[86]

General Barton ordered the 8th and 22nd Infantry Regiments to consolidate, while the 12th moved between them. This gave each regiment a more reasonable front to cover. It was, however, too late. All the units had suffered so many casualties, particularly in company officers, that they were hollow shells. Pedro Cano's "C" Company, for example, had only forty four men. Many were wounded or killed by artillery or mortar fire before replacements could get to their location.

There was little contact with the enemy on the following day, November 26th. Enemy units of the 1057th and 1058th Infantry Regiments remained purely in a defensive position. The enemy regrouped their forces for further defense while their artillery harassed 8th Infantry troops. The troops had a breathing spell. Although the enemy continued to use extensive artillery against their front lines, 8th Infantrymen were able to obtain a degree of rest prior to resuming intensive fighting. The 2nd and 3rd Battalions each sent a patrol along the front. Additional patrols from the 3rd Battalion contacted the 24th Cavalry on their right flank. While the 24th Cavalry Squadron established a platoon on the right flank of the Regiment, Pedro's 1st Battalion relieved the 2nd Battalion and moved into the line at 1445. The engineers continued their unbroken efforts to establish further supply routes to the forward units in preparation for operations, during which the 8th Infantry would move on toward open ground.[87]

On November 27th and 28th, the 8th Infantry maintained a defensive line opposing enemy positions. Elements of the German 942nd and 984th Infantry Regiments continued to defend strategic positions opposite the Regimental Sector. They delivered artillery, mortar and sporadic machine gun fires upon our troops. As the enemy regrouped its forces, relieved some combat units in the line and prepared to intensify its defensive action to screen the development of successive lines of resistance, the 8th Infantry sent patrols out to establish outposts, capture prisoners and determine the extent of any changes in enemy status or deployment. On the 27th, the 1st Battalion sent a strong patrol to the south of the position occupied by Company B. There, they met with heavy small arms fire from well-established positions further to the south. Pedro's Company C then sent a combat patrol to coordinate 045404 where it encountered a large group of enemy infantrymen. Having encountered Germany infantry at several points, the 3rd Battalion Patrols drove them back into their own lines and continued approximately 800 yards toward the east without meeting further German resistance. A short time later, patrols from the 1st and 3rd Battalions made contact with each other at coordinate 043415 where they cleared a substantial area along the Regimental Front of enemy personnel.[88]

Private Bill Loy of Company "C" recalled shooting near the ground or behind a tree and then being spotted by a German. When the Germans spotted them, they would of course shoot at them. When bullets passed near their ear, they would make a loud pow sound and hurt their ears. They would hear ping, pow, ping, pow and would listen for where the ping came from to shoot at the enemy. Usually the enemy would be hiding behind a log or stump and could not be seen. But when many men returned fire in the same direction, sometimes the German soldier would get scared and start running. That was one of the ways the Americans were able to kill a few German soldiers. Bill also recalled that some men sacrificed their life by placing dynamite under barbed wire and getting blown up, too. One soldier was wounded trying to blow up the barbed wire. Apparently he didn't feel as if he would make it out alive so he slid under the barbed wire with a stick of dynamite and both were blown up. Bill said this was only one example of the many sacrifices made by a multitude of brave men.[89]

On the following day, November 28th, the 8th Regiment once more sent aggressive patrols along the front. The 1st Battalion maintained contact with the 24th Cavalry Squadron, during which new, well-prepared enemy positions were discovered near a Y in the road which the Germans had previously blocked. Apparently they felt it would be the focal point of an 8th Infantry attack, coordinate 056431. The 3rd Battalion sent a patrol to contact the 4th Calvary Squadron through an area occupied by hostile troops at several points. After the patrol had returned, they had obtained information more clearly defining the location and deployment of the enemy. They fired mortars into this area in an attempt to dislodge the enemy at these points. They felt this new information would help them harass the enemy and support subsequent advances by 8th Infantry units. During the early part of the day, a Company I outpost suffered a heavy enemy counterattack. After a short effective fire fight, Company I repelled the enemy attack, inflicting many casualties upon them with rifle fire. In the afternoon, the 2nd Battalion relieved the 3rd Battalion on the front line. Engineers, continuing to work against time and under heavy fires, pushed supply routes ahead toward all battalion sectors.[90]

On the following morning, November 29th, when the Regiment was ordered to continue the attack, the 1st and 2nd Battalion started the attack, Pedro's 1st Battalion on the right and the 2nd Battalion on the left. The 3rd Battalion remained in Regimental Reserve. The 8th Infantry, opposed by the German 942nd Infantry Regiment, forged steadily ahead until the 1st Battalion, with Company B on the right and Pedro's Company C on the left. They met with heavy enemy small arms and machine gun fire. Both companies, pinned down and unable to move forward at coordinate 052432, pulled back at 1115 so that supporting artillery could plaster the enemy in this locality prior to a resumption of the drive. After the artillery had thoroughly covered these positions, Companies B and C were able to advance and achieve material gains. The 2nd Battalion, with Company G on the left and Company F on the right, met with stubborn enemy resistance and heavy artillery and automatic fires. They continued to advance until Companies F and G reached positions well forward of adjacent units at coordinates 049430 and 084432. As the attack progressed during the day, an increasing volume of enemy artillery, mortar and machine gun fire were delivered upon the troops. The enemy resisted stubbornly at every point of attack and only fell back when driven out of their emplacements by a combination of devastating forces which they could not withstand.[91]

On the morning of November 30th, Pedro's 1st Battalion attacked at 0845. The 2nd Battalion moved forward at 0900. Both Battalions immediately came under heavy small arms and machine gun fire. The enemy defended its position with increasing ferocity. When the 3rd Battalion was sent forward in the attack at 0930, it commenced moving from its assembly area to a position in the rear of the 1st Battalion. Supporting tanks thrust into enemy territory from a position between Companies A and B. A few minutes later, when the enemy launched a counterattack, Company B fought desperately to push the enemy back. The Germans, attacking in force with rifle

The aftermath of German Hurtgen Forest tree burst shelling.

grenades and rocket launchers were thrown back. In spite of heavy enemy fire, the 3rd Battalion advanced to the south and came abreast of Pedro's 1st Battalion. Coordinated advances by tanks and infantry pushed the enemy back at many points. However, the enemy resisted at other points with increasing fury. At 1640, the Regiment started to dig in for the night after a day of the bittersweet type of fighting.[92]

By December 1st, the enemy had reinforced units opposing the 8th Infantry. As these German units prepared to increase the tenacity of their defense, they delivered increasingly heavy artillery and mortar fire upon the 8th Infantry Sector to a depth of approximately 500 yards. They laid additional mine fields and other obstacles at strategic locations leading to their defensive lines. The 8th Infantry continued the tack to the northeast. Pedro's 1st Battalion attacked the enemy at 0818, and the 2nd Battalion at 0845. During the initial advance towards strongly defended enemy positions held by German elements of the 942nd Infantry Regiment and 353rd Replacement Battalion, both battalions met fierce small arms, machine gun, mortar and artillery fire. Pedro's 1st Battalion encountered a dense anti-personnel mine field at coordinate 050428 which delayed the progress of the attack in this sector. At 1130, the 3rd battalion was sent in between the 1st and 2nd Battalion sectors. Encountering mounting German resistance the 2nd Battalion was able to advance only a short distance. Pedro's Company "C" pushed ahead over difficult terrain against heavy German fire and innumerable obstacles. They reached a forward position at coordinate 053427. Company "A", was positioned on the right flank of Company "C" and on the left flank of the 3rd Battalion a short time later. After desperate offensive fighting by the 8th Infantry troops, the enemy was forced to withdraw approximately 400 yards from the center of the Regimental Sector during the day. The 8th Infantry had advanced through heavy defensive fire, covered mine fields, anti-personnel mines and obstacles along roads and other routes of advance. Combat engineers worked in close support of advancing troops during the entire day. They kept roads and trails cleared, swept mines and removed obstacles which reinforced current defense lines. This impeded the progress of the 8th Infantry with delaying action and the Regiment consolidated its gains and awaited further orders.[93]

Heroes

On the 2nd of December, 1944, elements of Germany's 942nd Infantry Regiment, 353rd Field Replacement Battalion and 353rd Artillery Regiment offered determined resistance against all attempts to dislodge them. At 0830, the 3rd Battalion started their Hurtgen Forest attack and advanced through heavy artillery fire, which fell throughout its zone of action. Pedro's 1st Battalion and 2nd Battalion moved forward at 0900, although Pedro was not among them.[94]

In an earlier 0800 departure, Private Pedro Cano had advanced with the assault elements of his Company C (1st Battalion) during an attack against strong German defenses in the Hurtgen Forest, near Schevenhutte, Germany. When his platoon was pinned down by two hostile machine guns covering a minefield, Cano, armed with a rocket launcher, ran through the intense machine gun fire to the right flank of his company. Although Cano had no knowledge of where the mines were planted or how dense the minefield was, he crawled through this dangerous area for a distance of twenty-five yards over rough, thickly wooded ground which afforded him little cover and scant visibility, and which was crisscrossed by deadly automatic fire. Cano crawled forward to a point within ten yards of the first enemy machine gun and fired his rocket launcher (bazooka) directly into the enemy emplacement. This reduced the hostile position, killing two gunners and five supporting riflemen. Private Cano then fired at the second German machine gun emplacement from the same position, killing two more gunners and forcing five supporting riflemen to withdraw. His actions permitted Company C to advance.[95]

Private Francisco G. Delgado of Company C was also advancing with the assault elements of his company against bitter enemy resistance when they became pinned down by machine gun fire which covered an enemy minefield through which Company C had to advance to reach its objective. Confronted by intense crossfire from two machine guns, the assault platoon of Company C suffered nine casualties, a number which threatened to increase unless the machine gun emplacements were immediately reduced. Private Delgado, with no knowledge of the density of the minefield or the location of the mines, crawled with his BAR through direct machine gun fire across the minefield over rough wooded ground for a distance of twenty yards. When he reached a position fifteen yards from the first hostile emplacement, he fired a burst from his weapon which killed the two hostile gunners and several supporting riflemen. Private Delgado then obtained a rocket launcher from a comrade who had followed his path into the minefield. He crawled another fifteen yards through point blank fire, and then fired his rocket launcher directly into the second German machine gun nest, destroying the gun and killing two gunners. Private Delgado discarded the rocket launcher and again procured his BAR and a number of hand grenades. He then crawled toward a group of eight enemy riflemen who were twenty-five yards distant, firing on them as he advanced. He rose to his feet when he was ten yards from the enemy and charged the position, throwing grenades and firing his BAR. He was thus able to kill six Germans and capture two. The reduction of the enemy's supporting riflemen permitted Private Delgado's company to continue its advance to a position eight hundred yards forward of this point, where a defensive line was established for the remainder of the day and night.[96]

Meanwhile, Company K came abreast of Company C on the left flank and was pinned down by withering crossfire from two additional hostile machine guns. Private Cano, aware of Company K's difficulty, crossed his own company's front and, after determining the position of the German guns, approached them stealthily from the flank. He crept forward through Company K's zone of action until he reached a point fifteen yards from the hostile machine guns. Firing one rocket from his rocket launcher, Private Cano reduced the nearest gun and killed two gunners. He then single-handedly reloaded his bazooka, normally a two man function, and fired at the second enemy machine gun from the same position, which destroyed the gun and killed two more gunners.[97]

At 1445, Companies C and K at last broke through the enemy line, but not until after having encountered desperate fighting from reinforced enemy units in well prepared positions. Companies C and K were able to advance quickly once this line was broken. They reached 056426, where they tied in for the night, while Company A moved up on the right of Company C. Company I, after a determined attack, overran well defended enemy positions and captured a large number of prisoners. Although the enemy had been able to hold its flanks, he was forced to withdraw at the center of his line under the decided pressure of the attack.[98]

On the following day, December 3rd, the 8th Infantry was opposed by elements of the enemy's 8th Parachute Regiment and elements of the 353rd Infantry Division. The enemy counter-attack was directed against the right flank of the Regiment and was preceded by an intense artillery and mortar barrage of approximately 300 rounds.[99] The 2nd Company of the German 8th Parachute Regiment launched a powerful counter-attack against positions held by Pedro's 1st Battalion of the 8th Infantry.[100]

The American advance resumed at 0830. Five hundred yards forward of the previous day's action, Private Pedro Cano's Company C jumped off in the attack and was pinned down in a pine forest by a deadly crossfire from eight enemy machine guns. Private Cano, still armed with a rocket launcher, crawled forward in the face of this heavy fire over terrain which afforded him neither adequate cover nor visibility to a position fifteen yards from the first gun. Private Cano fired a rocket at the first enemy machine gun, which destroyed the gun and killed two gunners. Private Cano then crept ten yards toward the second gun and, having reached a point fifteen yards from the weapon, again fired his rocket launcher. He destroyed the second machine gun, killed two gunners and again, single-handedly reloaded his weapon, a feat normally done by two persons. Private Cano then crawled another fifteen yards through heavy rifle fire toward the third gun. Having reached a point twenty yards from the third enemy machine gun, he fired directly into it, destroying the gun and two gunners. This daring action was largely instrumental in further timely advances of Company C toward its objective.[101]

The 8th Infantry attack jumped off with the 1st battalion on the right and the 3rd battalion on the left, and moved toward HAF HARDT at 1030, but at 1105 the forward battalions were ordered to assume a position along a favorable defense line. The 2nd battalion, which had been in reserve, was directed to defend its position with one company and assemble the remainder of the battalion at 048425. The 1st and 2nd battalions then sent aggressive patrols to the south at 1230 to prepare to destroy all enemy south of their positions in an area extending to the Regimental boundary. These patrols made contact with the enemy at 055419.[102]

During action on the same morning, Private First Class Francisco G. Delgado's and his Company C again encountered heavy machine-gun fire and became pinned down during the initial phase of its advance. Private Delgado crawled forward over rough, densely wooded terrain through direct fire for a distance of fifteen yards with his BAR. Reaching a point fifteen yards from the enemy machine gun nest, he fired a burst from his BAR into the enemy emplacement and its supporting defenses, which killed the two hostile gunners and supporting riflemen.

Private Delgado's heroic acts were personally witnessed by Odis L. Malone, Company C 2nd Lt., 8th Infantry. Lt. Malone recommended Private Delgado for the Distinguished Service Cross.[103]

2nd Lt. Malone also personally witnessed Private Cano's heroic acts on December 2nd and 3rd. It was 2nd Lt. Malone who originally recommended Private Cano for the Distinguished Service Cross, which was later upgraded to the Medal of Honor in 2014.[104]

During Company C's assault on December 3rd, 1944, Private First Class Wayne L. Johnson of Cosmos, Minnesota, was seriously injured on the Duren-Schvenhutte Road. Johnson had been among those who had come ashore on Utah Beach on June 8th, 1944, near the end of the initial wave of Allied troops. He was previously injured on July 18th, 1944, and sent to an army hospital in England. He received the Purple Heart for wounds received as a result of enemy action at this time. He had rejoined his company during the Liberation of Paris and marched down the Champs Elysees. On December 4th, 1944, he died as a result of the injuries he sustained on December 3rd. This man was a brave and capable soldier and a true hero. He had

No 25 PFC Wayne Johnson, Company C, 8th Infantry Regiment, 4th Infantry Division.

fought his way through France and into Germany, entering the Huertgen Forest on November 16th, 1944. PFC Wayne L. Johnson and Private Pedro Cano had fought together since the D-Day invasion. These men undoubtedly knew each other, having fought side by side from the beginning. To know their story is to remember their sacrifice. And to remember their sacrifice is to honor their memory. PFC Johnon's great-granddaughter, Jennifer, wrote a paper about about him, noting Wayne's letters sent home during the war. "Had to leave my love and give my life for my country," he wrote in one letter. In another: "Oh, I wish this war was over so I can think about coming home again." This theme is repeated in another letter: "Well, it's the same old story, it's just hard to think of what to write. There's a lot to write in one way but I just can't because I want to get back home again." By November 1944, constant battles had him longing even more for home: "I sure would like to be home again. I have seen enough of the world now." Wayne was buried in a military cemetery in Henri Chapelle, Belgium. In 1947, his remains were repatriated to Fort Snelling, Minnesota, his final resting place.[105] It has always comforted me to know that Pedro Cano was surrounded by good and honorable and brave men like Francisco Delgado, Wayne Johnson and Bill Loy.

Although the enemy assaulted the 8th Infantry position with decided vigor, the punch was quickly taken out of their drive and they were pushed back. Outposts were established at 051420, 052421 and 056422 to secure a line from which an attack could be launched on the following day.[106] Two days of fighting, December 2nd and 3rd, seem to shift the fight, and the German front lines in the Hurtgen Forest would not be the same from that day forward.

December 4–10, 1944, Hurtgen Forest Battle

On December 4th, the 1st and 2nd Battalions were ordered to attack at 1000 to mop up the enemy in an area to the right of their position and south to the 12th Infantry boundary. The main enemy body, consisting of elements of the 8th Parachute Regiment and elements of the 353rd Infantry Division, continued to hold their defensive line opposing the 8th Infantry. One reinforced company from the 1st Battalion and two reinforced companies from the 2nd Battalion commenced the attack on schedule. The 1st Battalion on the left and the 2nd Battalion on the right moved forward along a stream (coordinate 055422) until Companies A and F were brought under heavy small arms fire. Company E on the right was able to continue forward and outflank the enemy, and with supporting pressure from Companies A and F, the German lines were shattered at this point, which resulted in the capture of many prisoners. This attack had inflicted an element of surprise upon the enemy which caused appreciable disorganization among German troops and materially influenced timely progress of the 8th Infantry units. German artillery fire continued to harass their troops during the day but diminished in intensity by comparison to what had been experienced during previous operations. Several enemy fighter planes passedover the Regimental sector during the day but caused little damage. One of them was shot down at 1600. The 1st and 2nd Battalions, having reached their objective at the 12th Infantry Boundary at 1230, had organized their positions for planned defense through the night. But at 1615, these units were ordered to return to previous sector. The 4th Reconnaissance Troop placed one platoon at coordinate 056421 and another platoon at coordinate 057417 after the area had been cleared of the enemy, and established outposts at points unoccupied by friendly troops on the right flank of the Regiment. The 3rd Battalion continued to hold a position on the left flank of the Regiment. Company L was relieved by a platoon of the 24th Cavalry Reconnaissance Squadron. Twenty-nine German soldiers—captured during the day's operations and later questioned by their IPW Team—evidenced rather a low degree of morale.[107]

On December 5th, the Regiment held an aggressive defense line and organized the main line of resistance along its front. Elements from the 8th Parachute Regiment and 353rd Infantry Division continued to occupy their defense lines and harass 8th Infantry troops with artillery and mortar fire. 8th Infantry patrols were sent to the front and flanks of the Regiment. Pedro's 1st Battalion occupied the right half of the Regimental sector and the 3rd Battalion held the left half of the line. The 2nd Battalion was in reserve. 1st Battalion patrols established contact with the 24th Cavalry on the right and 3rd Battalion patrols made contact with the 4th Cavalry on the left. No enemy action was observed in either of these areas. The weather, cloudy with scattered rains, obscured observation. Later in the day, a 3rd Battalion patrol observed six German soldiers moving about, apparently on patrol, and having been observed by the enemy (coordinate 056433) drew mortar fire. Pedro's Company C and Company E were moved into an assembly area (coordinate 011416) for a twenty-four hour rest, which would give the troops an opportunity to clean up after a long period of rigorous, sustained combat.[108]

Private Bill Loy recalled that quite often Company C would get down to very few men, sometimes as few as 30, after starting at about 180 men strong. Most losses were due to battle casualties. They still had to hold any ground gained. Replacements would be sent in and they would fight another 3 or 4 days and then wait for more replacements. That's how the war went in the Hurtgen Forest. They would get one day of rest about every nine days, where the men would be pulled back to a rest area. There they would heat some water

Private Bill Loy, Company C, 8th Infantry Regiment, 4th Infantry Division.

in their helmets and drop all their clothes in the snow and then take a bath out of their helmet. Usually their faces and hair would be covered in mud and they could hardly be recognized. They were covered in mud from crawling in the melted snow or wet terrain. It seemed like it rained or snowed every day. Eventually a jeep would drive up loaded with food. They would be served half a turkey or half a chicken, a meal that the hungry men found very delicious. So once the jeep showed up they were always well fed. Bill recalled that as they would be eating their meal the men would be told they'd be moving back to the front shortly. This always caused the men to stop eating and dump their food and wipe their mess kit. They would then go somewhere and sit alone because it was always a bad feeling knowing you were heading back to the front line. Bill Loy recalled once have that pain go through him, but a few moments later he told himself he was going to be okay. So they would return to the front and make contact with the enemy. It would be the same thing, over and over.[109]

On the following day, December 6th, the Regiment was ordered to continue the defense of the main line of resistance and send patrols to both front and flanks. The enemy, still opposing the 8th Infantry with elements of the 8th Parachute Regiment and miscellaneous units of the

Hurtgen Forest.

353rd Infantry Division, continued to occupy their defense lines and fired intermittent artillery and mortar fire into the 8th Infantry sector. Pedro's 1st Battalion continued to hold the right half of the Regimental sector and the 3rd battalion still occupied the left half. A 1st Battalion patrol encountered Germans at coordinate 058427, and a 3rd Battalion patrol encountered the enemy at coordinate 056431. Both patrols immediately withdrew to their battalion areas. At 1100, Companies F and I were withdrawn to an assembly area for a 24 hour rest period. In the early afternoon, at 1400, a ten-man German patrol, having made contact with the 8th front lines, was driven back by mortar fire. The enemy took little other offensive action during the day and apparently prepared to improve his defense lines, which at this time consisted of well dug in positions, reinforced and protected by logs and earth. Meanwhile the enemy increased artillery and mortar activity against the 8th Infantry lines, but the effectiveness of this fire diminished by comparison to that of the previous day.[110]

On the morning of December 7th, the 8th Infantry was ordered to continue the defense of the main line of resistance, and, as on the previous day, send patrols to both front and flanks. Elements of the enemy 8th Parachute Regiment continued to oppose their troops. The 1st Battalion patrol established contact with the 24th Cavalry (coordinate 051434), but encountered no enemy troops. Another 1st Battalion patrol, moving aggressively to the front, made contact with the enemy (coordinate 057426) and then withdrew into the Battalion area. A 3rd Battalion patrol, moving to the front, made contact with the enemy, and having observed groups of Germans improving their defensive lines, withdrew while heavy American concentrations of artillery and mortar fire were placed at these points. Enemy activity increased as the day progressed. Several enemy patrols contacted Company A and another German patrol moved into Company B's sector, but both companies quickly repulsed these penetrations. Harassing enemy artillery and mortar fire diminished somewhat, causing but a few casualties among 8th Infantry troops during the day. Four prisoners taken by 8th Infantry patrols stated that the average age of the paratroopers opposing the 8th Infantry was approximately 19 years and also said that most German troops opposite the Regimental sector had not had drinking water for three days.[111]

On December 8th, the Regiment continued to defend its main line of resistance with the 1st Battalion on the right, the 3rd Battalion on the left, and the 2nd Battalion in Regimental reserve. A 1st Battalion patrol established contact with a platoon of the 4th Reconnaissance Troop on the left flank. There was no enemy encountered by either patrol. A 1st Battalion patrol, which was sent to the front a short time later, did observe some enemy activity (coordinate 058429). Another 3rd Battalion patrol, moving toward German positions, discovered the enemy at 055430. Both patrols withdrew into their Battalion areas and furnished supporting artillery and mortars with sufficient information to place heavy accurate fire on these positions. The enemy restricted offensive activity during the day to harassing artillery and mortar fires directed at the 8th Infantry front and continued to improve defensive lines in anticipation of further attempts on the part of American troops to break through their lines.[112]

On the following day, December 9th, the enemy out posted and improved their defense lines. They continued to deliver mortar and artillery fire upon the Regiment front, while the 8th Infantry again defended the main line of resistance with two battalions abreast. The 1st battalion held a position on the right and the 2nd Battalion on the left, with the 3rd Battalion initially in reserve. The 3rd Battalion relieved the 2nd Battalion on the left, the relief being completed by 1100. The 1st Battalion sent patrols to establish contact with the 24th Cavalry Squadron at 1345 and again at 1545. On the latter mission, the 1st Battalion patrol reported large groups of enemy soldiers digging in at 065417. A 1st Battalion reconnaissance patrol reported artillery firing from a clearing (coordinate 064426) at 1400 hours and later encountered small arms fire at a fire break north of the creek. A short time later, a 2ⁿᵈ Battalion patrol encountered machine gun fire at 056437. Hostile artillery employed interdictory fire upon their roads, observation posts and gun positions. Concentrations were small and shifted rapidly. Six rounds fell in the vicinity of Cannon Company, ten rounds near Service Company and thirty rounds on a crossroads (044423). A bridge (052429) was placed under fire and later troops and targets of opportunity were engaged.[113]

On December 10th, the Regiment supported the attack on the 83rd Infantry Division, which had moved into the Hurtgen Forests to relieve the 4th Infantry Division. The 8th Infantry fired mortars and small arms for the purpose of diverting the attention of the enemy and redirecting possible enemy fire away from the attacking force, which was to launch its advance farther to the south. Meanwhile, German units opposing the 8th Infantry lines remained in defensive position, firing artillery and mortar into the Regimental sector. There was a definite increase in the intensity of enemy artillery fire into the sector during the early part of the day, which indicated that the diversionary tactics of the 8th Infantry in support of the 83rd Division's attack had been successful. At 1100, approximately a battalion of German infantry was observed moving northeast from HOF HARDT. This battalion was slaughtered with artillery fire. Patrols were sent to the front by each American battalion to determine the location of the enemy defense line and any change which might come about in the enemy situation. The 1st Battalion patrol reached a position (coordinate 064426) where it observed abandoned hostile emplacements and many enemy dead. This patrol then moved toward the south to (064424) and from this point observed enemy infantry and one vehicle. A 2ⁿᵈ battalion patrol moving East (from 054429 to 060428) discovered three abandoned bunkers and was fired on at (064425). A 3rd Battalion patrol, moving out along the front, received mortar fire and observed a small group of enemy (06054245). As the 83rd Division prepared to relieve the 8th Infantry Regiment, which was the last unit of the 4th Division remaining in the Hurtgen Forest, the enemy was thought to be preparing to break contact and establish a defensive line East of the Roer River. The enemy line was becoming more thinly spread and it was likely that the Germans were shifting large numbers of troops from the defenses opposing the 8th Infantry to reinforce the area which was already under attack by elements of the 83rd Division. Enemy planes dropped flares over the Regimental sector at 1715, but, as on previous nights, took no offensive action.[114]

Pedro's 8th Infantry Regiment Departs Hurtgen Forest to Luxembourg

The relief of the 8th Infantry at its advanced position in the Hurtgen Forest by the 329th Infantry Regiment commenced at 0745 on the morning of December 11th. The Regiment had been in contact with the enemy for twenty-six consecutive days, during which it had experienced the most bitter fighting of its entire participation in the campaigns on the continent. For a period of sixteen days without rest or relief, the 8th Infantry had constantly pushed the enemy back over difficult terrain, through dense woods, and over natural obstacles. The enemy had had approximately two months in which to prepare extensive defenses, mine fields, tank ditches, road blocks, bunkers and fields of fire. During the bitterly contested advances of the 8th Infantry through the Hurtgen Forest, six German Infantry Regiments plus miscellaneous separate units fought tenaciously from prepared defense lines, but were badly mauled by the ferocity of the American attack. Of the six regiments opposing the 8th Infantry, five were so battered that they were forced to be replaced in rapid succession. The enemy, in keeping with his policy of counterattacking after being pushed from each position regardless of losses, launched eight counterattacks in force to regain lost ground, all of which were repulsed with heavy casualties. During the Regiment's advance through the Hurtgen Forest, 484 German prisoners were captured and a large number of Germans were killed. Although the 8th Infantry had received many casualties itself, due to the difficult terrain and the character of the enemy defense, the Regiment was nevertheless able to complete its mission.[115]

By 1400 on December 11th, the relief of the 8th Infantry in the Hurtgen Forest had been completed. The Regiment moved to assembly areas prior to departure for Luxembourg, where it would hold a defense line against light German opposition, which would give the troops some degree of rest and would enable the Regiment to be regrouped and retrained. Meanwhile, elements of the German 8th Parachute Regiment and 942nd Infantry Regiment continued to deliver artillery fire on an area forward of the position held by their troops. Little damage was done and casualties were insignificant.[116]

The Regiment left its assembly area on December 12th at 0800 on the following morning by motor for Luxembourg.[117]

The Hurtgen Forest battle was over for Private Pedro Cano and the 8th Infantry Regiment. But the war continued.

The Regiment assumed defensive positions opposing enemy elements of the 999th Training Battalion and 320th Infantry Regiment, which were thought to be securely emplaced in concrete fortifications on the other side of the Moselle River. The 1st Battalion held the right half of the Regimental Sector and the 3rd Battalion assumed a position on the left. The 2nd Battalion was in reserve. In taking over these positions, the 1st Battalion had relieved elements of the 22nd Infantry at 1915 and the 3rd Battalion had relieved elements of the 12th Infantry at 1810.[118]

On the 15th of December, the Regiment continued the defense of its sector with Pedro's 1st Battalion on the right, the 3rd Battalion on the left, and the 2nd Battalion in reserve. The enemy maintained defensive lines opposing the 8th Infantry and harassed their lines with light artillery fire. The 1st and 3rd Battalions improved their defensive positions, and all other groups not engaged in tactical activities utilized their time for the improvement of their billets and cleaning of weapons and equipment.[119]

By the morning of December 16th, the position of the Regiment had become more firmly established. The 8th Infantry was opposed by the German 44th Festung Battalion. German troops increased their mortar and artillery fires early in the day, delivering several heavy concentrations in both the 1st and 3rd Battalion sectors. Late in the day (at 2030), the enemy sent a five man patrol along the 1st Battalion front which was quickly repulsed by Company B. Meanwhile, all troops not actively engaged in the defense of the Regimental sector devoted their time to the care of their equipment, which had been severely used during the Hurtgen Forest engagements. The Medical Detachment, located at SENNINGEN, conducted physical examinations and provided immunization shots for some of the troops. Troops took showers, when able. During the evening, it was reported that the enemy was counterattacking across the Sauer River and had established a bridgehead opposite the 12th Infantry front. The 8th Infantry was alerted for a possible thrust by these enemy forces south into their sector.[120]

On the morning of December 17th, the German troops opposite the 8th Infantry remained in their defensive position but greatly increased the extent of their artillery fire, the largest concentrations falling in the 3rd Battalion area. To the north and on other fronts, the tempo of the enemy advance became a full-blown offensive. The Regiment, under alert, held its position with Pedro's 1st Battalion on the right, 3rd Battalion on the left, and the 2nd Battalion in reserve. The 2nd Battalion, alerted to move on one hour's notice, was attached to a task force commanded by Colonel James S. Luckett, and prepared to relocate to a position where it could strengthen the threatened area. The 2nd Battalion with attachments (Company A, 70th Tank Battalion, less 1 platoon, and battery B, 29th Field Artillery Battalion) was given notice that it would move to the threatened area by motor at 0910. By 1500 the battalion had arrived in the sector into which the Germans were driving and was fully prepared to support the defense of this area. One bomb fell in the Regimental area but caused no damage. Meanwhile the enemy was thought to be preparing to increase the tempo of his drive in areas adjacent to the Regimental sector, and the Regiment quickly readied itself for this probability.[121]

The Regiment held the same position on the following day, December 18th, with two battalions, the 1st Battalion on the right, and the 3rd Battalion on the left. The 2nd Battalion was still part of the task force assigned to strengthen the 12th Infantry area, against which the Germans were exerting heavy pressure. The 1st and 3rd Battalions spent the entire day improving their positions, establishing road blocks, mines and booby traps at points where the enemy was most likely to attempt to break through the 8th Infantry lines. Elements of the German 44th Festung Machine Gun Battalion and the 58th Festung Battalion continued to occupy their old line, from which they delivered harassing artillery fire, the largest concentration falling in the northern part of the 8th Infantry sector. Again, as on the previous day, enemy planes flew over the area but no offensive action was taken.[122]

On December 19th, the Regiment was still opposed by the 44th Festung Machine Gun Battalion and other unidentified units. The enemy continued to harass the Regimental line with moderate concentrations of mortar and artillery fires and sent several small reconnaissance patrols into the 8th Infantry section on the right and the 3rd Battalion on the left. Those battalions continued to hold their positions. Both battalions made further improvements in their frontal defense by establishing additional road blocks, booby traps, trip flares, and laying more mines. Each battalion held a company in reserve: A for the 1st Battalion and I for the 3rd Battalion. The 2nd Battalion had not been released from Task Force Luckett and was still bolstering the defense of the area threatened by enemy penetration. All 8th Infantry personnel not actively engaged in defensive operations were instructed in field training, physical conditioning and adjustment of artillery.[123]

The War Ends for Pedro Cano

On December 20th, Private Pedro Cano was declared a non-battle casualty. He was evacuated to a hospital in England.[124] The war was effectively over for Pedro, but the scars of endless battles would last for the rest of his life.

Private Cano was returned to the United States and placed in an army hospital in Waco, Texas. Around March 26, 1946, Pedro Cano was released from the Veterans Hospital in Waco, Texas, and came home to his wife, Herminia, and small daughter, Dominga.[125]

Pedro Cano Receives Distinguished Service Cross in the Mail

On March 27, 1946, Pedro received a Distinguished Service Cross in the mail, accompanied by an official citation from the War Department and a terse letter. That was all. The citation told Pedro's story. One day in December, 1944, as Private Cano's Company C, 4th Infantry Division, was advancing through Germany when it encountered severe resistance from German machine gun emplacements. Carrying a bazooka, Cano crawled forward through a heavily infested minefield under a hail of fire and reached a point within 10 yards of the closest enemy position. He fired one rocket into the emplacement, killing two gunners and five riflemen. Then he crawled farther and fired again, killing two more machine gunners and an indefinite number of riflemen. A short time later, a neighboring rifle company also ran into trouble. So Cano crawled over to help. He got within 13 yards of the machine gun position and fired. Two more gunners were killed. With two more rounds he killed two German machine gun emplacements. The next day he eliminated three more machine gun emplacements. The total for the two days was seven machine gun emplacements and almost 30 enemy soldiers killed.[126]

Cano's commanding officer thought he should have the Silver Star and told Cano so. The Silver Star medal is the United States Armed Forces' third-highest personal decoration for valor in combat. The officer changed his mind several days later, however, when Pedro's platoon was surprised by seven German soldiers, who demanded their surrender. Cano calmly tossed a hand grenade into their midst, which surprised the Germans. All seven Germans were wounded. After that heroic act, 2nd Lt. Odis Malone decided Cano should be recommended for the Distinguished Service Cross.[127]

Cano heard no more about the medal until he received it in the mail on March 27th. He showed it to a few friends, who decided that the U.S. Army had forgotten something: No one had pinned the medal on Pedro's chest! Cano's war veteran friends felt he had been "slighted" by the army by what they called a "callous disregard for the proprieties connected with such an honor." In the entire military history of the United States of America, no man had ever received the Distinguished Service Cross in the mail. This became a national scandal and was reported by newspapers throughout the entire nation.[128]

Local American Legion Post officials got busy. They drafted a message to the U.S. Army's Eighth Service Command requesting that it do something about a military ceremony for Private Pedro Cano.[129]

Meanwhile, on March 27th, Pedro went up to the Red Cross to show Mrs. Camila Bader, county Red Cross secretary, a letter he received from the Adjutant General's office at Washington, D.C. Pedro couldn't read English very well, and he wanted to know if the letter needed an answer.[130]

The letter in question was from the Adjutant General himself, Major General Edward F. Witsell. It read: "I have the honor to inform you that by direction of the President the Distinguished Service Cross has been awarded to you by the Commanding General, Third United States Army." Then the citation was listed. "The decoration," the letter continued, "will be forwarded to the Commanding General Eighth Service Commander, Dallas, Texas, who will select an officer to make the presentation. The officer selected will communicate with you concerning your wishes in the matter."[131]

Mrs. Bader made a copy of the letter, which she brought to the Edinburg Valley Review. Meanwhile, five veterans working at the American Legion sat around and talked about what a good story it would be. They had a hard time finding Pedro, but they finally did locate him. They knew Pedro had killed more than 30 Germans single handedly and had destroyed seven enemy machine gun positions in two days of fighting. They heard his modestly told story. It was learned that the Distinguished Service Cross had gone from the Eighth Service Command to the Harlingen Army Air Field. A Lieutenant there mistakenly asked Pedro if he wanted a ceremony to be awarded the "Purple Heart." It is unknown why the Lieutenant confused the Distinguished Service Cross for the Purple Heart. Regardless, Pedro said he already had that medal.[132]

That was that until he took the letter to Mrs. Bader. Telegrams went from the Review to Senators W. Lee O'Daniel and Tom Connally and Congressman Milton H. West. They said, "WE OF THE EDINBURG VALLEY REVIEW AND AMERICAN LEGION ARE TRYING TO RECTIFY WHAT IS CONSIDERED AS A SLAP IN THE FACE TO MEXICAN CITIZEN PEDRO CANO, A DISABLED VETERAN OF THE U.S. ARMY. CANO RECEIVED A DISTINGUISHED SERVICE CROSS FOR HEROIC ACTION AGAINST THE GERMANS THROUGH THE MAIL ACCOMPANIED ONLY BY A TERSE NOTE AND CITATION. WE FOUND OUT ABOUT IT AND ARE DETERMINED THAT PRESENTATION OF ARMY'S SECOND HIGHEST AWARD SHOULD BE MADE AT SUITABLE CEREMONY. URGENTLY REQUEST YOU CONTACT WAR DEPARTMENT WITH DEMAND FOR WAINWRIGHT'S PRESENCE. A COMPARABLE MEXICAN OFFICIAL WILL BE IN ATTENDANCE. ALTHOUGH WE WERE NOT OFFICIALLY PROTESTING AWARD OF DSC, HIS CITATION REVEALS ACTS MORE HEROIC THAN MANY CONGRESSIONAL MEDAL WINNERS. WE BELIEVE CEREMONY WILL BE IMPORTANT IN CEMENTING GOOD INTERNATIONAL RELATIONS BETWEEN BORDER TOWNS ON BOTH SIDES. APPRECIATE IMMEDIATE ANSWER."[133]

As stated above in the telegram, it needs to be pointed out that it was painfully obvious to all that Pedro Cano's heroic actions merited the Medal of Honor. But that fight would have to wait for another 70 years.

Although Pedro was born in La Morita, Nuevo Leon, Mexico, he had lived his entire life in South Texas. Some have claimed that he did not receive the Medal of Honor due to being born in Mexico. Yet there have been hundreds of Medal of Honor recipients born in another country going all the way back to the American Civil War. Past Medal of Honor recipients have been born in Scotland, Wales, England, Italy, Germany, Canada, Switzerland, Isle of Man, France, Denmark, Australia, Italy, Norway, Czech Republic, at sea (English Channel), Poland, Spain, Blegium, India, Sweden, Hungary, Barbados, Mexico (Civil War), Bohemia, Finland, Austria, Philippines, Netherlands, Serbia, Croatia, Turkey, China, Slovakia, Montenegro, Mexico (including WW 2 recipient Marcario Garcia, before Pedro Cano), Guadeloupe, Saint Vincent, Malta, Barbados, Cuba, Bermuda, and Montserrat.

Although a Medal of Honor can be awarded only to members of the U.S. armed forces, being a U.S. citizen is not a prerequisite for eligibility to receive the medal. Since the American Civil War, hundreds of people born outside the United States have received the medal. The large number of foreign-born recipients during the 19th and early 20th centuries was mostly due to immigration waves from Europe.[134]

The first answer came from Sen. O'Daniel, and read: "TELEGRAM RECEIVED AND AM TAKING IMMEDIATE ACTION WILL ADVISE YOU LATER TODAY." The later wire that afternoon read: "IN FURTHER REFERENCE YOUR TELEGRAM, HAVE DISCUSSED MATTER WITH PUBLIC RELATIONS BRANCH. DIRECTIVE IS BEING SENT TO SAN ANTONIO AND PROPER CONTACT WILL BE MADE FOR CEREMONY INCIDENT TO PRESENTATION OF AWARD. AM INTERESTED IN MATTER AND WOULD BE GLAD TO KNOW WHEN DETAILS HAVE BEEN WORKED OUT. SPECIALLY URGED THAT PRESENTATION BE MADE BY GENERAL WAINWRIGHT HIMSELF."[135]

Sen. O'Daniel sent a special messenger with a letter to Maj. Gen. W.B. Persons, Chief Liason Division of the War Department. That letter quoted the original telegram from Edinburg. To that he added, "General Wainwright is located at San Antonio, Texas, and would be available for each ceremony, and I know that such a tribute to the citizens of our neighboring Republic on the South would have a salutary effect. I urgently request that such action be taken."[136]

The second answer came from Sen. Connally. It read: "TELEGRAM RECEIVED RE PEDRO CANO. HAVE DISCUSSED MATTER WITH WAR DEPARTMENT WHICH IS LOOKING INTO MATTER. HOWEVER THEY ADVISE MUST HAVE HIS SERIAL NUMBER AND HIS ARMY ORGANIZATION."[137]

An answer with that information went back. It read: "CANO ARMY SERIAL NUMBER 38360348. HIS COMBAT ORGANIZATION WAS CO. C, 8th REGT. 4th INFANTRY DIV. THIRD U.S. ARMY. WAR DEPARTMENT APPARENTLY ONLY MILDLY INTERESTED. SUGGEST YOU CONTACT STATE DEPARTMENT. CITIZENS OF THIS COMMUNITY HIGHLY EMBARRASSED OVER SITUATION. NORTHERN MEXICO OFFICIALS ARE EMBARRASSED AND INSULTED OVER APPARENT MISTREATMENT OF MEXICAN CITIZEN. HIGHLY IMPORTANT GEN. WAINWRIGHT HIMSELF APPEAR AT CEREMONY TO EASE SITUATION. NO ONE ELSE CAN SATISFY OUR NEIGHBORS ACROSS THE BORDER AND U.S."[138]

Then came Sen. Connally's answer: "FURTHER BE TELEGRAM PEDRO CANO WAR DEPARTMENT INFORMS ME THAT GEN. WAINWRIGHT HAS DISPATCHED A STAFF OFFICER TO EDINBURG TO CONFER WITH LOCAL CITIZENS WITH REGARD TO THIS MATTER."[139]

Then came Cong. West's answer: "REC'D TEL WAR DEPARTMENT CALLING GENERAL WAINWRIGHT HEADQUARTERS LONG DISTANCE INSTRUCTING THEM TO COMMUNICATE WITH YOU WITHOUT DELAY REGARDING AWARD MADE TO PEDRO CANO. DEPARTMENT ASSURED ME THAT OFFICER OF PROPER RANK WILL MAKE THE AWARD. IF NOT HANDLED TO YOUR SATISFACTION PLEASE ADVISE. WILL APPRECIATE YOUR RELAYING THIS INFORMATION TO THE AMERICAN LEGION."[140]

The next day another wire from Cong. West: "WAR DEPARTMENT ADVISES CASE OF PEDRO CANO LOCATED YESTERDAY IN NEW YORK. IT HAD BEEN SENT TO EIGHTH SERVICE COMMAND DALLAS WITH NO RECORD IN WASHINTON WHICH OCCASIONED DELAY. AM INFORMED DALLAS OFFICE SENT INQUIRY TO CANO GIVING HIM CHOICE OF TWO CEREMONIES OR MAILING OF DECORATION. CANO SELECTED LATTER AND DECORATION MAILED TO HIM IN ACCORDANCE WITH HIS REQUEST. PLANE LEFT GEN. WAINWRIGHT'S HEADQUARTERS THIS MORNING AND GENERALS PERSONAL REPRESENTATIVE SHOULD BE IN YOUR OFFICE NOW MAKING ARRANGEMENTS FOR CEREMONY."[141]

As previously stated, perhaps their plans were to offer Private Pedro Cano the choice of either a ceremony or having the decoration mailed to him, but all it takes is one fella with a personal prejudice or indifference to change their plans. As stated earlier, it was learned that the Distinguished Service Cross had gone from the Eighth Service Command to the Harlingen Army Air Field. A Lieutenant there asked Pedro if he wanted a ceremony to be awarded the "Purple Heart." Pedro said he already had that medal. According to Pedro Cano, no offer was ever made of a Distinguished Service Cross, a finding the army would establish as fact when their investigation uncovered all the facts to their satisfaction. They agreed that a proper Distinguished Service Cross ceremony honoring Pedro Cano was in order.

Cong. West also received a wire from R.B. McLeaish, general manager of the Valley Planning Board. It read: "CITIZENS OF EDINBURG

INDIGNANT OVER FACT DISTINGUISHED SERVICE CROSS SENT PEDRO CANO IN MAIL WITH CITATION AND NO CEREMONY. WE AGREE WITH THEM IN FEELING THAT IT WOULD GREATLY HELP OUR INTERNATIONAL RELATIONS IF RANKING OFFICER HAD BEEN DELEGATED TO PRESENT CROSS TO HIM WITH SOME CEREMONY. WOULD APPRECIATE YOUR CONTACTING WAR DEPARTMENT AND REQUESTING IF POSSIBLE GENERAL WAINWRIGHT BE DELEGATED. WILL ARRANGE CEREMONY. IF DONE BELIEVE IN ADDITION HELPING GOOD NEIGHBOR POLICY WOULD BOLSTER MORALE ENLISTED MEN IN SERVICE."[142]

McLeaish also wrote Gen. Wainwright requesting that he come for the presentation. J. Loy Ramsour, commander of the Edinburg American Legion Post, wrote the Eighth Service Commanding General Walton H. Walker. He set out the facts and requested a high ranking officer for the ceremony. Gen. Walker replied in part, "I have taken this matter up with the War Department and have been informed that arrangements have been made for General Jonathan M. Wainwright to present this award. I further directed one of my staff to communicate informally with the Headquarters, Fourth Army, where it was ascertained that General Wainwright has tentatively selected the morning of April 25 to visit Edinburg and make the award. Inasmuch as the Fourth Army is at present a separate command, I would suggest that any further correspondence concerning this case be addressed to the Command General Fourth Army, Fort Sam Houston, Texas, marked to the attention of Brigadier General L.B. Kelser."[143]

And that's how it all happened.[144]

State Sen. Rogers Kelly found out that one of Cano's chief desires was to obtain American citizenship, so Kelly said that he would begin naturalization proceedings as soon as possible.[145] During the campaign through Europe, Pedro said he once asked his commanding officer about citizenship. His commanding officer agreed that Pedro should be a citizen but said that "we're too busy right now with the Germans."[146]

Pedro was a farm laborer in Hidalgo County before the war and he still desired to farm. The war left him disabled and unemployed, but he received a pension from the government. Pedro hoped to farm a small tract about 30 acres in size. Sen. Kelly talked with friends about the matter and endeavored to find a plot that would suit Pedro's needs.[147]

Edinburg was looking forward to celebrating Cano's heroic actions and his decoration in the proper manner. "We want to show him our great regard for his extraordinary feats," said J. Loy Ramsour, American Legion Commander. "Pedro doesn't speak English very well," said State Senator Kelly. "Maybe the army didn't understand that he would have appreciated the honors customary in receiving such a high decoration."[148]

Meanwhile, Cano's long promised citizenship proceedings were underway. Although Cano had lived in Texas since he was only two months old, the 25-year-old Hidalgo County farmworker never had been naturalized.[149]

An application of citizenship was completed by Senator Rogers Kelly on March 30, 1946 and forwarded to Charles Lonergran, in charge of the Immigration and Naturalization service in the Brownsville District Court, with a request that it be considered in the May term of Federal Court. This was the only step necessary, Kelly said, in naturalizing a World War II veteran who had served overseas.[150]

Pedro Cano became a naturalized citizen of the United States on May 16, 1946.[151]

Sen. Kelly also requested Rio Farms, Inc. to consider Cano's application for a farm and tools from the giant cooperative. In a letter to H.A. Hodges, the senator stated it was his understanding "that this is the reason for the existence of Rio Farms, Inc. By that I mean your organization was chartered for the purpose of assisting extremely worthy cases such as this one." He further stated that although Cano received total disability pay from the army of $115 per month, it was still Pedro's desire to farm and earn his own living. The application requested a house for Cano, his wife, Hermina, and small daughter, Dominga, a second-hand car and machinery to operate the farm, "either in the form of a monetary loan or by some other means."[152]

War Dept. Investigates Army Blunder

Col. George R. Beane was in Edinburg, Texas, making an investigation of the "army blunder" in awarding the Distinguished Service Cross to Private Pedro Cano. Also investigating was Col. John T. Morgan, assistant inspector general to the Eighth Service Command in Dallas, Texas. Both officers said "an unfortunate error had been made and the army is anxious to rectify it by offering a general officer to make the presentation."[153]

Morgan and Beane, representing the Army Service Forces and Army Ground forces respectively, agreed with the insistence of the people of Edinburg that Gen. Wainwright's Fourth Army headquarters would furnish the general officer. "To rectify an oversight and error, we will be satisfied only if General Wainwright himself makes the presentation," Ramsour said. "After all, he is only 250 miles from here and could handle the situation in half a day on a date selected by him."[154]

"I am not empowered to guarantee Gen. Wainwright's presence," Beane said. "I am not his aide but secretary to his general staff. After verifying the facts, which I have done to my complete satisfaction, I can only recommend that he attend."[155]

General Wainwright Agrees to Distinguished Service Cross Ceremony

General Jonathan M. Wainwright confirmed he would present the second-highest Army award to Pedro Cano, modest Edinburg hero, at 11 a.m. Tuesday, April 23, officials of the American Legion and the Chamber of Commerce announced. Lt. Col. George R. Beane, who visited Edinburg, acknowledged the appointment for Wainwright in a telephone conversation with J. Loy Ramsour, commander of the local American Legion post.[156]

At a meeting of the Chamber of Commerce special events committee, the date and time were selected and a steering committee to make detailed arrangements for the all-day celebration was named. "Now that General Wainwright has accepted, there's every reason for Edinburg having the biggest celebration of its kind in history," Chamber of Commerce chairman Keener Hudson said. The chairman noted that other valley heroes would also be invited to participate in the ceremony, as well as high Mexican and American government officials.[157]

The committee chairman for the Pedro Cano celebration met with Army officials to continue plans to honor Edinburg's unsung hero, and were informed that the date General Wainwright would be in Edinburg for the presentation had been changed to April 25th. The Chamber of Commerce also made plans for raising $2500, which would be necessary to stage the celebration.[158]

The chamber voted to have the fete on the courthouse square on April 25th. They named Allan Engleman, Edinburg Valley Review publisher, to go to San Antonio for a conference with the general's staff to set the exact time and make the necessary arrangements for carrying out the program as the Bataan hero Wainwright wished.[159]

The plan was for a welcoming committee to meet Wainwright and his party at Moore Field and escort them to Edinburg. Other United States officials, to be selected later, would be in the party. Mexican officials or commensurate were to be invited.[160]

On that day a barbeque would be held for the official parties, the four bands to appear in the parade, the local business men who contributed the $2500, and all veterans and their wives from the county. Edinburg would be decorated within an inch of its life by a professional firm to welcome the 10,000 visitors expected in town for the fete.[161]

The finance committee for Pedro Cano's celebration on the courthouse square on April 25th started collecting $2500 to stage the affair, according to orders issued by Chairman R.G. Yingling. At the meeting of the group, including both Anglo and Latin Americans, captains for the four quarters of the town, the outlying sections, the courthouse and the packing sheds were named. A roll call of the 23 committee-men at the meeting netted $650 in a few minutes. Should there be any money left over, it would go to Edinburg's unsung hero if the wishes of the finance committee were followed. All checks were to be made payable to the Cano Fund. A special account was set up by chamber member Harry Cook, and he accepted checks or cash donations at the chamber office. The Latin Americans agreed to raise $1000 and the Anglo Americans $1500. The money was to be deposited in the bank and a treasurer was to disperse the funds, according to the committee members.[162]

Cano Day Schedule, April 25, 1946

11:30 a.m. – Parade will move out from the Missouri Pacific depot on E. Harriman. Order of parade: Highway patrol; American Legion color guard, cars of distinguished guests; U.S. Navy band; Veterans of all wars; McAllen High School band; Nurses Aides; Girl Scouts; Edinburg High School band; Boy Scouts; Sergeanettes; float.

12:00 p.m. – Ceremony of presentation of Distinguished Service Cross medal to Private Pedro Cano by General Jonathan M. Wainwright and introduction of other guests by Sen. Rogers Kelley, master of ceremonies.

12:45 p.m. – Open house to be arranged by a women's committee.

1:00 p.m. – Barbeque at Kiwanis park for parade participants, all veterans and all donors.

2:30 p.m. – Reception at Country Club for distinguished visitors. Admission by invitation only.[163]

Proclamation

WHEREAS the citizenry of Edinburg and Hidalgo county are gathering today to honor Pedro Cano; and

WHEREAS a committee of Edinburg citizens have spent many hours at work to arrange for appropriate recognition of the heroism of this son of Hidalgo county; and

WHEREAS there will be many guests of Edinburg from out of town to aid in properly commemorating this day; and

WHEREAS several notable war heroes and their entourages will be here to join in the eulogization of this man; and

WHEREAS these visitors will include Gen. Jonathan Wainwright and Adm. J.J. Clark; and

WHEREAS PEDRO CANO will be presented the Distinguished Service Cross, be it therefore

PROCLAIMED THAT YOU, the citizenry of Edinburg, Hidalgo County, Texas, do proper honor to this Edinburg hero, Pedro Cano, who won the second-highest combat medal awarded by our government, by marking well this day in his honor.[164]

W.D. Woodroof
Mayor

1946 Distinguished Service Cross Ceremony: Gen. Wainwright pins medal on Private Pedro Cano.

Wainwright Pins Distinguished Service Cross on Pedro Cano

The entire hubbub about the Distinguished Service Cross was a bit confusing to Pedro Cano but he took it with a grin. In the first place, Pedro wasn't sure whether he was a private or a private first class when he ended two years of army service. He was promised a promotion, but he wasn't quite sure whether he got it.[165]

Also confusing was the award of the Distinguished Service Cross. He received it by mail, then a couple of colonels from San Antonio, sent to investigate the matter, took it home with them pending a formal award. Of course Pedro eventually got the Distinguished Service Cross medal back on April 25th, when Jonathan M. Wainwright pinned it on his chest.[166]

Cano, his wife, Herminia, and small daughter, Dominga, moved to a small white house at Monte Cristo, three miles north of Edinburg. Of all the people interested in his "battle of the DSC," Pedro appeared to be the least excited. "We just got into some fighting," was Pedro's explanation of the Hurtgen Forest affair in which he won the nation's second-highest military award. "There were two of us, a boy from Los Angeles and I. He was promised the DSC, too. I don't know whether he got it." It is believed the other boy was Private First Class Francisco G. Delgado, who indeed was also awarded the DSC. His actions are described in the December 2nd and 3rd battle accounts found earlier in this book.[167]

The opening event was the arriving by air of Gen. Jonathan M. Wainwright and a party of army officials from San Antonio, Rear Admiral J.J. "Jocko" Clark and a group of naval officers from the Corpus Christi Naval Air Station, and a delegation of Mexican Army authorities headed by Gen. Eulogio Ortiz, Monterrey, Mexico, Commanding General of the 7th military district. Wainwright, Clark, Ortiz and their parties rode with Cano.[168]

The ceremony got underway officially at 11:30 a.m. with a parade consisting of the official visitors and hundreds of Edinburg and valley residents moving from the Missouri Pacific depot up East Harriman Street toward the public square at the Hidalgo County Courthouse. The ceremony was expected to last less than an hour. Edinburg business owners closed their doors from 11 a.m. to 1 p.m. in tribute to Cano. Flags and bunting were placed in downtown Edinburg to add to the dignity of the occasion. School children were granted a controlled holiday which permitted them to attend the ceremony.[169]

On the reviewing stand with the Army officers and government officials were Pedro Cano's mother, Ms. Nicolas G. Cano, his wife, Herminia, daughter Dominga and Mexican Consular authorities.[170]

Private Pedro Cano, the modest 25-years-old Edinburg resident who slew over 30 Germans in the Hurtgen Forest near Schevenhutte, Germany, in December 1944, stood with Gen. Jonathan M. Wainwright before a crowd of approximately 6000.[171]

In a short address before pinning the Distinguished Service Cross medal on the honoree, Wainwright said, "I am without words to thank the people of Edinburg for the sincerity and hospitality of our welcome today. Many times I have been in the Rio Grande Valley, from Brownsville to El Paso. I know every foot of it. I hope to be back often. I was especially thrilled at the sight of young children who lined the streets."[172]

Wainwright continued, "I left Washington by plane only 12 hours before I arrived here. I had been called to Washington for a conference with the

Pedro Cano in uniform.

Secretary of War. I was asked to stay a few more days but replied I must go to Texas and I would make it unless my plane broken down. Here I am, deep in the heart of Texas."[173]

Wainwright continued, "I feel that I am highly honored in being privileged to present to such a gallant soldier this second-highest decoration of our country," Wainwright told the cheering crowd.[174]

Speaking extemporaneously, he said the citation was one of the finest he had ever read, and that Cano should have possibly received, "a higher award [the Medal of Honor], but that is beyond my control."[175]

Little did General Wainwright know that his firm belief that Pedro Cano deserved the Medal of Honor would become reality almost 70 years later.

This was a rare moment in American history indeed. A Medal of Honor recipient (Gen. Wainwright) was presenting the Distinguished Service Cross to a future Medal of Honor recipient.

Lt. Col Beane, aide to Wainwright, read the Third Army citation detailing Private Pedro Cano's two-day feat, where he estimated 30 German soldiers were killed and seven German machine gun positions were knocked out by Cano during the campaign in Western Germany in December, 1944.[176] The citation is as follows:

"For extraordinary heroism in connection with military operations against an armed enemy in GERMANY. On 2 December 1944, the infantry company with which Private Cano was advancing near SCHEVENHUTTE, GERMANY was halted by intense enemy machine-gun fire. Armed with a rocket launcher, Private CANO crawled through a heavily mined area, under a hail of fire, and reached a point within ten yards of the nearest emplacement. He fired a rocket into the position, killing the two gunners and five supporting riflemen, fired into a second position, killing two more gunners, and with hand grenades killed

Edingburg, Texas, Distinguished Service Cross Ceremony, 1946.

several and dispersed other protecting riflemen. Then, when an adjacent company encountered heavy fire, Private CANO crossed his company front, crept to within fifteen yards of the nearest enemy emplacement and killed the two machine-gunners with a rocket. With another round he killed two more gunners and destroyed a second gun. On the following day when his company renewed the attack and again encountered heavy machine-gun fire, Private CANO, armed with his rocket launcher, again went forward over fire-swept terrain and destroyed three enemy machine-guns in succession, killing the six gunners. His daring actions without thought of his own safety permitted the advance of his company. His conspicuous heroism, and his fearless determination and courageous devotion to duty exemplify the highest tradition of the military service."[177]

Then Wainwright with a firm hand clasp pinned the medal upon the hero's breast. Asked to make a speech, Cano stood modestly at the edge of the stand and said on receiving the nation's second-highest military award: "Thank you, everybody."[178]

Preceding Wainwright, Rear Admiral J.J. "Jocko" Clark, was introduced by State Senator Rogers Kelley as "the greatest sea going fighter in the history of the United States Navy." Clark characterized the ceremony as "symbolic of the mutual good relationship between the United States and Mexico." Clark said, "I hope we never have another war, but if we do I am sure we will find these two great republics fighting side by side in the cause of freedom."[179]

High Mexican army officials, including Gen. J. Trinidad Rodriguez, commander of the Reynosa Matamoros military sector, and Col. J. Tiburco Garza Zamorra, Reynosa area commandment, witnessed the ceremony. Speaking briefly in Spanish, Rodriguez tendered to Wainwright the regrets of Gen. Eulogio Ortiz, Monterrey, commander of the seventh Mexican military district, at being unable to attend the ceremony, and also congratulated Cano for "the heroic actions for which you are being decorated."[180]

Also preceding the award, state commander Herman G. Nami, San Antonio, of the American Legion, presented Cano with a life membership. "I wish also to congratulate you merely for being alive after your experiences."[181]

Two other Congressional Medal of Honor winners besides Gen. Wainwright, Sergeant Jose M. Lopez, Brownsville, and marine Sgt. Billy Harrell of Mercedes, and a Distinguished Service Cross recipient, Staff

April, 1946, Edinburg, Texas, Distinguished Service Cross ceremony parade.

Sergeant Julian Gonzales, Edinburg, sat on the reviewing stand as private Cano was decorated.[182]

A number of short speeches were given by Edinburg citizens, with Allan Engleman, publisher of the Edinburg Valley Review, leading off the program. He spoke of Cano as "the bazooka man with as much punch as his weapon," and traced the history of Cano Day.[183]

Edinburg Legion Commander J. Loy Ramsour and Mayor W.D. Woodroof spoke briefly, welcoming the guests to the city, including Lauro Izaguirre, Mexican Consul at McAllen.[184]

Cameras were numerous as spectators sought to obtain snapshots of Wainwright. One Edinburg miss won a smile and a nod from the general, who sat at attention during the speeches to pose for her. A number of persons were sitting in the courtroom windows overlooking the reviewing stand, many dangling their feet from the roof. A ripple of laughter ran through the crowd during one speech when a Boy Scout perched in a tree grasped the limbs hastily after a long noise indicated his resting place might crash onto the stand.[185]

A parade in which Boy Scouts, Girl Scouts, a navy band and local school bands participated preceded the presentation. The crowds cheered loudly as the notables came riding by, followed next in line by Cano's car.[186]

April, 1946, Edinburg, Texas, Distinguished Service Cross ceremony parade.

Pedro Cano Killed in Accident

Pedro Cano was killed on June 24, 1952, when his pickup was in a head on collision with a car driven by James S. Kidwiller (McAllen), about two miles north of Pharr on Highway 281. Pedro was thrown out of the pickup. He was survived by his wife, Herminia, two daughters, Dominga and Mary, ages 9 and 5, a son, Susano, 2-1/2 years, his mother, Nicolosa Cano, and a half-sister, Alvina.[187]

Pedro Cano Buried with Military Honors

On June 28, 1952, former comrades in arms paid their last tribute to a hero of World War II, Pedro Cano, recipient of the Distinguished Service Cross medal for his outstanding gallantry in that conflict. An Honor Guard of four men, assigned to that duty by Lieut. R.W. Byrd of Harlingen Air Field Base, guarded the body of Pedro Cano as it lay in state at the family home.[188]

A military truck of Company I, 112th Armored Cavalry, transported Pedro's remains to Sacred Heart Catholic Church for the service. After Rev. Fr. Jerry Meagher had completed the service, a detachment of Company I, 112th Armored Cavalry of the Texas National Guard, provided an escort of honor. The pallbearers included friends and former comrades from the Edinburg American Legion and veterans of Foreign Wars posts. The pallbearers were Joe Avila, S.M. Cardenas, Leonard Stewart, J.J. Poinboerf, Louis Kroupa, Tom Simmons, Charles Flores and Ralph Hinojosa. Pedro was buried in Hillcrest Memorial Park with military honors.[189]

Texas Legislative Medal of Honor

WWII hero Pedro Cano was posthumously honored with the Texas Legislative Medal of Honor at a ceremony in Edinburg, Texas, on May 18, 2010.

But like anything else in life, there is a story behind this event. Aaron Pena of Edinburg, Texas, was in mourning over the loss of his 16 year old son, John Austin. His son had gone to a party and was given a drug that killed him and two other gentlemen. It was devastating for Aaron, who spent a lot of time at the cemetery. He would take his lunch, breakfast and even dinner at the cemetery. Basically he was out there all of the time.

Motivated by the pain of his son's death and his search for meaning, Aaron ran for the legislature, because he did not like the rise of drugs and cartels and their influence on his community. Aaron won his race and was elected to the legislature. Rep. Pena became drawn to people whose lives were lost tragically, because such stories were similar to his circumstance. He felt that Hispanics who served in the military were under-recognized, and even treated as second-class citizens.

In his discussions with veterans, some of the old-timers told Aaron Pena about Pedro Cano's huge Distinguished Service Cross ceremony in 1946. He began asking questions about Pedro and his story. During his daily visits to the cemetery he came across Pedro Cano's grave. Aaron thought it was a remarkable coincidence that the same time the old-timers were telling him about Pedro Cano he came across Pedro's grave. He felt the grave was not kept up to the standards deserved for someone who had exhibited so much valor in his life.

Rep. Pena continued searching for information on Pedro Cano but couldn't find very much. In time, his search led him to the local museum, where he found photos and old articles about the 1946 medal ceremony. He discovered how Pedro had received the Distinguished Service Cross in the mail. He learned about how Pedro desired to become a U.S. citizen. His focus on honoring Pedro Cano now became an obsession, so he instructed his staff to research Pedro Cano's story. They looked for WW2 veterans to hear their memories about Pedro, and researched where Pedro's family now lived.

Every two years in Texas, the Texas Legislative Medal of Honor is bestowed on a worthy soldier. Rep. Pena felt driven to honor Pedro Cano. He felt as if Pedro's life had been brought to his attention. A powerful member of the military advisory committee wanted to select someone else, but Rep. Pena persisted. Perhaps it was his continued search for meaning after the loss of his own son, but he felt spiritually driven to get Pedro Cano honored. His efforts eventually succeeded, and Pedro Cano was selected as the next recipient of the Texas Legislative Medal of Honor in 2010. I came across a Texas article on Pedro Cano Day and contacted Rep. Pena's office. Contact between the Cano family and Texas government was once again fully established. I sent Rep. Pena photos of Pedro Cano that he was not aware of and the public had never seen. I connected his office to Pedro's children, Dominga, Mary and Susano.

This honor was extremely important to the Cano family. Rep. Pena and his faithful assistant, Mari De Leon, remembered this unsung hero, Pedro Cano, at a time when no one else did. The Cano family was deeply touched by their efforts, so four years later when the President called

May 18, 2010, Edinburg, Texas. Texas Legislative Medal of Honor ceremony: L-R Stephen Cano, Mary Arias, Governor Perry, Alvina Martinez, Rep. Aaron Pena.

to let the family know that Private Pedro Cano would receive the Medal of Honor, Pedro's daughter, Dominga, made a very specific request to me (Stephen) that we get both Aaron and Mari into the Medal of Honor ceremony. I made the call to the U.S. Army and the Cano family was blessed to have them join us for the Medal of Honor ceremony in Washington, D.C.[190]

Rep. Aaron Pena authored HCR5, the legislation that conferred the medal to the Edinburg soldier for heroic actions performed in service of country.[191] Governor Rick Perry presented the medal to the Cano family at the Edinburg Municipal Auditorium. "I am so proud the State of Texas has elected to recognize the bravery of Pedro Cano. More than a namesake for a road and an elementary school, this unassuming soldier from Edinburg exemplified the best in all of us. From the humblest of beginnings, he was one of our greatest," said Rep. Aaron Pena in a statement.[192]

Governor Rick Perry praised the late World War II hero as "a young man who left this beautiful town to defend his adopted country and achieved far above and beyond the call of duty."[193]

Sen. Juan "Chuy" Hinojosa, D-McAllen said, "The 81st Legislature of the State of Texas hereby posthumously confers the Texas Legislative Medal of Honor on Pedro Cano in recognition of his courageous actions in World War II and express to his family its deepest appreciation on behalf of all his fellow Texans."[194]

Rep. Verónica González, D-McAllen, and Edinburg Mayor Richard García, also expressed words of thanks and appreciation.

Family member Stephen Cano (author) spoke words on behalf of Pedro Cano's family as follows:

Texas Medal of Honor Ceremony—Private Pedro Cano
Stephen P. Cano
May 18, 2010

First of all, I'd like to thank Governor Rick Perry, Senator Hinojosa, Representative Pena, Representative Gonzales and Mayor Garcia for your presence here today. Governor Perry, we realize you have many important matters on your agenda so we are grateful for your presence here today. Representative Pena, thank you for your hard work to make this day a reality. We appreciated the time spent with you yesterday and hearing about how Pedro Cano's cause became your cause. We would also like to extend our thanks to all of the other legislators who helped to make this day possible and our thanks also goes out to your staff for their hard work, too. I might add that I believe you bring honor upon yourselves for undertaking this noble cause because there is no greater cause than the calling to rise up and defend your country.

May 18, 2010, Edinburg, Texas. Texas Legislative Medal of Honor ceremony, Stephen Cano speaking.

Private Pedro Cano was an ordinary man thrust into an unordinary world war. The character of Private Pedro Cano would have been firmly established long before his heroic actions on the battlefields of Europe. I believe the community of Edinburg helped to shape young Pedro's heart and character. I think it's important for communities across America to always remember how much of an impact we have on our children. In order to support the family, Pedro would have started working hard as a young boy. Pedro's father Secundino and my grandfather Leandro came to Texas about the same time in 1920. My grandfather was a horseman for General Carranza in the Mexican Revolutionary War and would always sing Revolutionary songs while they worked in the fields of Texas. I'd like to think Pedro heard those songs and even sung them himself. Pedro would have enjoyed the simple things of life. Time spent with family, good Mexican food, his mother's handmade tortillas. There is a peace that comes from working on the land and I'm sure Pedro's heart was full of it.

But a dark cloud was soon to come over America and a great world war would soon engulf families across America, and Pedro's life as he knew it was about to change forever. The war in Europe stirred the hearts of Americans from West coast to East coast, from New York to Los Angeles and from DeMoine, Iowa, to Edinburg, Texas.

Pedro, out of love and devotion for the only country he ever knew, America, volunteered to join the U.S. Army in their fight against Hitler's Nazi regime. Lt. C Timothy Doolittle from WW2 fame once said there is "nothing as strong as the heart of a volunteer." Little did Pedro know that he would have a front row seat to some of the most historical and ferocious battles in world history.

It's been said "War is Hell" and the Hurtgen Forest battle certainly qualified as hell on earth. From November 3 – December 6, 1944, the 4th infantry division lost over 7,000 men. This was the equivalent of 10 members per company dying every day. Many if not all of Pedro's fellow soldiers would have certainly fallen in the Hurtgen Forest battle. War is cruel.

Pedro would come home a changed man. They say time heals all wounds, but Pedro would only have 6 more years to heal his wounds and make the most of his life. We can only look back at a life given in the service of his country, honor his sense of duty, pay tribute to his heroic actions beyond the call of duty and remember this unsung hero as a true American hero. I believe Pedro would be proud of his children, Dominga, Mary and Susano and his grandchildren and great-grandchildren. He would also have been proud of his sister Alvina and her family. Their character and gentle spirit are a testament to Pedro's life.

Today we honor a great American hero. An ordinary man thrust into an unordinary world war. It can truly be said he stood in our place so we could be free today because freedom is not free. For that reason, we honor him and will forever be in his debt.

Ronald Reagan once said, "Some people live an entire lifetime and wonder if they ever made a difference in the world." Well, Pedro Cano didn't have that problem because he made a difference for America. We are gathered here today not just to remember Pedro Cano, but we are gathered here today to honor Pedro Cano.

God bless the city of Edinburg, God bless the great State of Texas and God bless the United States of America. Thank you.

Stephen P. Cano
May 18, 2010, Edinburg, Texas

2002 Defense Authorization Act

In 2002, Congress through the Defense Authorization Act, called for a review of Jewish American and Hispanic American veteran war records from WWII, the Korean War and the Vietnam war, to ensure those deserving the Medal of Honor were not denied because of prejudice. During the review, records of several soldiers of neither Jewish nor Hispanic descent were also found to display criteria worthy of the Medal of Honor. The 2002 Act was amended to allow these soldiers to be honored with the upgrade, in addition to the Jewish and Hispanic American soldiers.[195]

In 2010 I contacted Lt. Col. Mike Moose, Spokesman for the Department of the Army Human Resources Command, and inquired if Private Pedro Cano was being considered for the Medal of Honor. The officer asked me to wait while he checked and a short time later in a surprised voice informed me that Private Pedro Cano was in fact being considered for the Medal of Honor. He said it was being reviewed by appropriate authorities and the review was still in progress. I was shocked. Almost 70 years had passed since Pedro received the Distinguished Service Cross in 1946. I was truly amazed and honored to be the first family member to find out about Pedro being considered for the Medal of Honor. I immediately advised my father, Alvaro, and called Pedro's daughters, Dominga and Mary, and son, Susano, to share the hopeful news.

President Obama Calls Pedro Cano Family

In May 2013, Pedro Cano's family received a telephone call from President Obama informing the family that after almost 70 years, Private Pedro Cano had been selected to receive the Medal of Honor. Dominga's daughter, Rosalinda took the call and was quite speechless during the conversation. Following is a press release by Dominga Perez, daughter of Pedro Cano.

February 19, 2014   PRESS RELEASE

My dad, Pedro Cano, was a humble man who worked hard at everything he did including being the best soldier he could be. He believed in America with all of his heart and was proud to be an American soldier and serving his country in her time of need.

He cared deeply about his family and that included the men he served with in Europe.

I would give anything to have my dad here today to personally receive this great honor. I was a child on the review stand in 1946 when General Wainwright pinned the Distinguished Service Cross on my dad. General Wainwright said he felt privileged to present such a gallant soldier the second-highest decoration of our country. Then upon reading the citation General Wainwright stated that Pedro Cano's citation was one of the finest he had ever read. Those words have comforted our family for decades.

A few months ago, President Obama called my family and spoke words that we have longed to hear in our lifetime. He said my father, Pedro Cano, had been approved for the Medal of Honor. We were deeply moved by his phone call and stand in awe of this great honor being bestowed upon Pedro.

Our family will forever be grateful to the men who served by Pedro's side in WW2. If my dad were here he would say he was just doing his duty defending his country and fellow soldiers. He was small and stealthy so the Germans had a hard time shooting him. But they tried. I remember hearing stories about him dodging behind trees and rocks to avoid their machine guns. My dad said they just ran into a big fight. The Hurgen Forest was the site of some of the most ferocious battles in Germany. My dad survived the war and came back to live his life in Edinburg, Texas. He died about 6 years later in a car accident.

We are grateful that our great nation has remembered this simple soldier from Edinburg, Texas. We look forward to sharing Pedro's story with America.

Dominga Perez (daughter of Pedro Cano)

A Letter to President Obama

I thought it was important that the President knew a little about Pedro's life so I (Stephen Cano) decided to write him a letter on Pedro's journey.

March 5, 2014
Dear Mr. President,

The Medal of Honor ceremony on March 18th is fast approaching. I look forward to attending the ceremony and meeting you and the wonderful families that are part of the Valor 24 men. Since our family will not be speaking at the Pentagon Hall of Heroes ceremony, I wanted to share some insight on Pedro Cano and some thoughts on his long journey that culminated in Pedro being a recipient of the Medal of Honor.

As a boy growing up in Edinburg, Texas, Pedro Cano lost his father at an early age. He worked hard to help support his mother and siblings. It wasn't easy but Pedro learned to appreciate a hard day's work and making an honest living. He was a gentle person and soft-spoken. It was very common to see him helping out in the neighborhood or playing his accordion or just fishing near a river. It was a close community and much of Pedro's identity was established during this time in Edinburg, Texas. This was his life. Those years would turn out to be the easy years.

As we all know, a dark cloud was soon to come over America and a great world war would soon engulf families across this great nation and Pedro's life as he knew it was about to change forever. The war in Europe stirred the hearts of Americans from West Coast to East coast, from New York to Los Angeles, and from Des Moines, Iowa, to Edinburg, Texas. And Pedro Cano would soon join the U.S. Army and be sent off to boot camp and shortly thereafter to Europe in the fight against Hitler's Nazi regime. Little did Pedro know that he would have a front row seat to some of the most historical and ferocious battles in world history. Pedro served his country with great distinction and bravery well beyond the call of duty.

He came home a changed man. War has a way of doing that. He was moody and easily angered at times and would have that thousand-mile look. But he was a humble man and never looked for special attention. Soon he received his Distinguished Service Cross in the mail, which created a mild uproar and eventually brought General Jonathan Wainwright to Edinburg, Texas, to personally present Pedro with the Distinguished Service Cross. During the ceremony in 1946, General Wainwright said Pedro Cano's citation was one of the finest he had ever read and that the award might have been higher, and I quote, "but that is beyond my control." Sixty-eight long years have passed since those words were spoken by General Wainwright. His words have comforted our family in the many decades that followed. But those words stirred a belief that this young brave soldier should have received the nation's highest military honor, the Medal of Honor. But the circumstances of the day were beyond Pedro's control and time moved on. And Pedro's story stood frozen in time. Remembered by a few and forgotten by most.

A few months ago our family received a phone call from you, Mr. President, and you spoke words we have longed to hear in our lifetime. You said Pedro Cano had been approved for the Medal of Honor. On March 18th, sixty-nine long years after Pedro's heroic acts on the battlefields of Europe, Pedro Cano will receive the nation's highest military award, the Medal of Honor. We are deeply grateful that Pedro is being recognized by the country. We are touched that his deeds from so long ago are still remembered by our nation.

We will forever be grateful to the men who served by Pedro's side in World War Two on the battlefields of Europe. When I think of the 4th Infantry Division and especially Pedro's 8th Infantry Regiment and the men of Company C, I think of the words of Stephen Spender's poem: "You are men who in your lives fought for life…and left the vivid air signed with your honor." Today we remember and honor the sacrifices made by those men.

Pedro would only live another six years after the war. Although we did not have the blessing of time with Pedro, we gladly share his story with you and all Americans across this great nation. Former President Ronald Reagan once said, "some people live an entire lifetime and wonder if they ever made a difference in this world." Well, Pedro Cano didn't have that problem because he made a difference for America.

It has been almost 69 years since WW2 ended. Some may feel resentment or anger over the long wait to recognize Pedro. It is no small matter to deny a Medal of Honor, so when it happens and it takes 67 years to correct the injustice...we remember Pedro's love and devotion and sacrifice for America. We remember that in the end, America did not forget this brave soldier. We will always remember that a grateful President, a grateful Congress, and a grateful Army gathered to honor Private Pedro Cano and the men who make up the Valor 24.

But let us remember this truth as well. "Where there is a brave man, it is said, there is the thickest of the fight, there is the place of honor." In that moment, when Pedro stepped forward to face the enemy in the Hurtgen Forest, in that moment, when Pedro crawled his way through the forest and took out seven German machine gun nests, in that moment when death was so near and yet he showed no fear, in that moment, a son, a husband, a father, a soldier, put his love of country above his love of life. Sixty-nine years ago Pedro had his place of honor. And on March 18th, Mr. President, a grateful nation will recognize that fact.

God bless you, Mr. President. God bless the men and women who serve in our armed forces and God bless the United States of America.

Very Respectfully, Stephen Cano

Medal of Honor Ceremony, March 18, 2014

Originally the ceremony was to take place in July 2013, but was delayed to November and then delayed again to March 2014. President Barack Obama

posthumously bestowed the Medal of Honor upon Private Pedro Cano at a ceremony on March 18, 2014, in the East Room of the White House. Pedro's eldest daughter, Dominga, accepted the Medal of Honor for her father.

Descendants of Pedro Cano joined other honorees'

Medal of Honor ceremony, White House Library: L-R Alec Cano, Nina Cano, Stephen Cano.

Medal of Honor ceremony, Dominga Perez and President Obama.

families at the White House ceremony. Pedro Cano family members included his daughter, Dominga Perez, grandchildren Salvador Perez, Armando Perez, and Robert Perez, great-grandchild Armando Perez Jr., second cousin Stephen Cano (author) and his wife, Nina Cano, and son, Alec Cano, (Stephen's) mother, Genevieve Cano, niece, Emily Lindsay, and family friends Aaron Pena and Mari De Leon.

President Obama awarded the Medal of Honor to 24 Army veterans in recognition of their valor during major combat operations in World War II, the Korean War, and the Vietnam War. Each veteran honored on March 18, 2014, had already received the Distinguished Service Cross—the nation's second-highest military award—but 19 of them were previously overlooked for the Medal of Honor due to their racial or ethnic backgrounds. The ceremony on

Medal of Honor ceremony. Front L-R: Mari De Leon, Aaron Pena, Dominga Perez, Alec Cano, Emily, Genevieve, Nina & Stephen Cano; back L-R: Armando Jr., Armando, Salvador, Robert Perez.

83

Medal of Honor ceremony, L-R: Armando Perez Jr., Armando Perez, Salvador Perez, Dominga Perez, Robert Perez, Stephen Cano.

March 18th followed a 12-year Pentagon review, ordered by Congress, of past discrimination in the military.

"No nation is perfect," the President said at the ceremony. "But here in America we confront our imperfections and face a sometimes painful past, including the truth that some of these soldiers fought and died for a country that did not always see them as equal."

At the ceremony the President awarded the Medal of Honor to three living veterans, and 21 other veterans received the honor posthumously. Following were the veterans honored at the ceremony.

Veterans honored posthumously:

* World War II veterans
  * Private Pedro Cano
  * Private Joe Gandara
  * Private First Class Salvador J. Lara
  * Sergeant William F. Leonard
  * Staff Sergeant Manuel V. Mendoza
  *Sergeant Alfred B. Nietzel
  *First Lietenant Donald K. Schwab
* Korean War veterans
  *Corporal Joe R. Baldonado

*Corporal Victor H. Espinoza
*Sergeant Eduardo C. Gomez
*Private First Class Leonard M. Kravitz
*Master Sergeant Juan E. Negron
*Master Sergeant Mike C. Pena
*Private Demensio Rivera
*Private Miguel A. Vera
*Sergeant Jack Weinstein
* Vietnam War veterans
　*Sergeant Candelario Garcia
　*Specialist Four Leonard L. Alvarado
　*Staff Sergeant Felix M. Conde-Falcon
　*Specialist Four Ardie R. Copas
　*Specialist Four Jesus S. Duran
Living veterans honored:
* Specialist Four Santiago J. Erevia
* Staff Sergeant Melvin Morris
* Sergeant First Class Jose Rodela

Each soldiers awarded on March 18, 2014, had been denied the Medal of Honor due to their Jewish, Hispanic or African American ethnicity. "So with each generation, we keep striving to live up to our ideals of freedom and equality and to recognize the dignity and patriotism of every person," President Obama said.

Medal of Honor ceremony. L-R Army Chief of Staff Gen. Ray Odierno, Alec Cano, Lt. Gen. William T. Grisoli, Nina Cano, Stephen Cano.

U.S. Army Reception

On March 17th, the U.S. Army hosted a wonderful reception dinner for family members attending the Medal of Honor ceremony. It was a chance to meet our military leaders and other families and enjoy a beautiful concert by the U.S. Army Chorus. My son, Alec, was able to talk drums with the U.S. Army drummer at the reception. This chance encounter led to Alec playing drums with the U.S. Army small band at the White House after the Medal of Honor ceremony.

Medal of Honor ceremony: Alec Cano playing drums with Army band.

Pentagon Hall of Heroes, Secretary of the Army John McHugh, Secretary of Defense Chuck Hagel, Dominga Perez, Army Chief of Staff Gen. Odierno, Sgt Major of the Army Chandler.

Medal of Honor Hall of Heroes Induction Ceremony

On March 19th, the Pentagon held a Medal of Honor Hall of Heroes Induction ceremony for the 24 veterans honored with the Medal of Honor the day before. Located on the Pentagon's main concourse is the Hall of Heroes, a room dedicated to the more than 3,460 recipients of the Medal of Honor, the United States' highest military decoration. There are three different versions of the Medal of Honor: the Army version, the Sea Service version (Marine Corps, Navy and Coast Guard), and the Air Force version. All three versions are displayed in the Hall of Heroes. Along the walls of the room are the names of each recipient.

Chief of Staff of the Army Gen. Ray Odierno said, "In the faces of our recipients and their relatives, we see the faces of 24 heroes. They are the faces of a diverse Army and a diverse America, faces that have shaped

Pentagon Hall of Heroes ceremony, Army Chief of Staff Gen. Ray Odierno presents medal to Dominga Perez.

our Nation's history, built this Nation's strength, and defended this Nation's security. Our Nation and our Army are strong because in every war, in every generation, men and women, citizens and immigrants, have raised their right hand to defend the Constitution of the United States. In doing so, they have committed themselves to a cause greater than themselves, to the ideals of this Nation."[195]

Secretary of Defense Chuck Hagel said the following: "Nearly 70 years ago, a Jewish chaplain who had just lived through the carnage at Iwo Jima led his fellow marines in dedicating a cemetery on that island. They were burying their friends and their comrades—men of all religions, all races, all creeds. In mourning them, he observed:

"Here lie officers and men [of all colors], rich men and poor [men]... [all together]. Here are Protestants, Catholics, and Jews...together. Here no man prefers another because of his faith, or despises [another] because of [their] color. Here there are no quotas of how many from each group are admitted or allowed. ...Thus do we memorialize those who, having ceased living with us, now live within us. Thus do we consecrate ourselves, the living, to carry on the struggle they began. Too much blood has gone into this soil for us to [ever] let it lie barren. Too much pain and heartache have fertilized the earth on which we stand. We solemnly swear: this shall not be in vain.'"

Secretary Hegel continued, "Today, on the doorstep of our nation's capital, we honor 24

Pentagon Hall of Heroes, Armando Perez Jr. and Armando Perez.

88

heroes with the same solemn pledge that was given on the island of Iwo Jima: that their sacrifice shall not be in vain. Thank you for what you have done for our country."[196]

At the end of the ceremony, all attending military leaders and Medal of Honor family members sang "The Army Song." It was a very moving experience and a fitting end to the events honoring the Medal of Honor recipients forever known as THE VALOR 24.

The Army Song

March along, sing our song, with the Army of the free.

Count the brave, count the true, who have fought to victory.

We're the Army and proud of our name!

We're the Army and proudly proclaim:

First to fight for the right,

And to build the nation's might,

And the Army goes rolling along.

Proud of all we have done,

Fighting till the battle's won,

And the Army goes rolling along.

Then it's HI! HI! HEY!

The Army's on its way.

Count off the cadence loud and strong;

For where'er we go,

You will always know

That the Army goes rolling along.

Pedro Cano Army Facts

Enlistment Date: November 28, 1942
Discharge Date: April 18, 1945
Regiment: 8th Infantry Regiment (1st Battalion)
Division: 4th Infantry Division
Company: Company C
Campaigns (5):
  Normandy 1944 (Arrowhead for D-Day Landing)
  Northern France 1944
  Rhineland 1944–1945
  Ardennes–Alsace 1944–1945
  Central Europe 1945
Training: Fort Meade, Maryland
Awards:
  Distinguished Service Cross 1946
  DSC upgraded to Medal of Honor 2014
  Purple Heart
  Bronze Star (V for Valor)
  European Medal for five campaigns
  World War II American Campaign Medal
  World War II Victory Medal

Return to the Hurtgen Forest

Shortly after the Medal of Honor ceremony I received a letter from Albert Trostorf, Mayor of Merode in Germany and also a WWII historian. Albert said his main expertise was in the Battle of the Hurtgen Forest during WWII. Merode is a small rural town at the northeastern edge of the Hurtgen Forest. Albert said he became interested in the battle when he met his first American veteran more than 39 years ago. Albert has made contact in the past with more than 600 World WarII veterans. Most of these brave men served with different units in the Hurtgen Forest. Most of them left the battlefields with wounds, and many of the veterans lost their friends in the battles.

According to Albert, from 1991 thru 2000 he organized annual "peace and friendship" reunions with both American and German WWII veterans. He said these events were always very emotional and that after so many

Visiting Hurtgen Forest area, where Pedro Cano fought on December 2nd and 3rd, 1944. L-R Stephen Cano, Alec Cano, Aaron Cano, Nina Cano (June 2016).

years the veterans of both nations were sitting side by side around the table and were talking about their WWII experiences and their families.

Albert offered to give Pedro Cano family members a guided tour of the Hurtgen Forest and to take us to the exact area Pedro Cano and Company C fought on December 2nd and 3rd, 1944. On June 6th, 2016, the Cano family returned to the Hurtgen Forest for the first time since Private Pedro Cano fought with the 8th Infantry Regiment from November to December 1944. Stephen Cano (author), Nina Cano (wife), and Alec and Aaron Cano (sons) visited the exact location (within 200 yards) of where Pedro Cano and Company C fought on December 2nd and 3rd 1944. It was surreal to see the trenches largely intact and we actually saw many artifacts on the ground. It was hard to imagine that such a peaceful forest was the site of some of the most violent fighting in Germany during WWII.

I attended my first WWII family reunion in Duren, Germany, in 2017 and found it to be a very moving experience and left with many new friendships. We had one American and one German WWII veteran attend the event. There were many children and grandchildren of WWII Hurtgen Forest veterans in attendance, too. I plan on going back to the reunion in 2018 and filming Pedro Cano's journey.

Endnotes

1. Balkoski, Utah Beach, p. 191
2. Balkoski, Utah Beach, p. 192
3. Balkoski, Utah Beach, p. 199
4. Balcer, Operations of the VII Corps., 1st U.S. Army In the landing on Utah Beach, Normandy, France 6 – 7 June 1944, p. 20-21
5. Balcer, Operations of the VII Corps., 1st U.S. Army In the landing on Utah Beach, Normandy, France 6 – 7 June 1944, p. 21
6. Moore, The Operations of Company C, 8th Infantry (4th Infantry Division) in the attack of the Hurtgen Forest, Germany, 19-21 November 1944, p. 6-7
7. Moore, The Operations of Company C, 8th Infantry (4th Infantry Division) in the attack of the Hurtgen Forest, Germany, 19-21 November 1944, p. 7
8. Moore, The Operations of Company C, 8th Infantry (4th Infantry Division) in the attack of the Hurtgen Forest, Germany, 19-21 November 1944, p. 8
9. Action Against Enemy Reports After/After Action Reports, period 1 November 1944 – 30 November 1944, p. 3
10. Action Against Enemy Reports After/After Action Reports, period 1 November 1944 – 30 November 1944, p 3
11. Action Against Enemy Reports After/After Action Reports, period 1 November 1944 – 30 November 1944, p. 3
12. Action Against Enemy Reports After/After Action Reports, period 1 November 1944 – 30 November 1944, p. 4
13. Action Against Enemy Reports After/After Action Reports, period 1 November 1944 – 30 November 1944, p. 4
14. Action Against Enemy Reports After/After Action Reports, period 1 November 1944 – 30 November 1944, p. 4
15. Action Against Enemy Reports After/After Action Reports, period 1 November 1944 – 30 November 1944, p. 4-5
16. Action Against Enemy Reports After/After Action Reports, period 1 November 1944 – 30 November 1944, p. 5
17. Action Against Enemy Reports After/After Action Reports, period 1 November 1944 – 30 November 1944, p. 5
18. Action Against Enemy Reports After/After Action Reports, period 1 November 1944 – 30 November 1944, p. 5
19. Action Against Enemy Reports After/After Action Reports, period 1 November 1944 – 30 November 1944, p. 5-6
20. Action Against Enemy Reports After/After Action Reports, period 1 November 1944 – 30 November 1944, p. 6
21. Action Against Enemy Reports After/After Action Reports, period 1 November 1944 – 30 November 1944, p. 7
22. Action Against Enemy Reports After/After Action Reports, period 1 November 1944 – 30 November 1944, p. 7
23. Action Against Enemy Reports After/After Action Reports, period 1 November 1944 – 30 November 1944, p. 7
24. Action Against Enemy Reports After/After Action Reports, period 1 November 1944 – 30 November 1944, p. 6-7
25. Moore, The Operations of Company C, 8th Infantry (4th Infantry Division) in the attack of the Hurtgen Forest, Germany, 19-21 November 1944, p. 11
26. Action Against Enemy Reports After/After Action Reports, period 1 November 1944 – 30 November 1944, p. 7
27. Action Against Enemy Reports After/After Action Reports, period 1 November 1944 – 30 November 1944, p. 7
28. Action Against Enemy Reports After/After Action Reports, period 1 November 1944 – 30 November 1944, p. 7-8

29. Action Against Enemy Reports After/After Action Reports, period 1 November 1944 – 30 November 1944, p. 8

30. Moore, The Operations of Company C, 8th Infantry (4th Infantry Division) in the attack of the Hurtgen Forest, Germany, 19-21 November 1944, p. 9-10

31. Moore, The Operations of Company C, 8th Infantry (4th Infantry Division) in the attack of the Hurtgen Forest, Germany, 19-21 November 1944, p. 10-11

32. Moore, The Operations of Company C, 8th Infantry (4th Infantry Division) in the attack of the Hurtgen Forest, Germany, 19-21 November 1944, p. 13

33. Moore, The Operations of Company C, 8th Infantry (4th Infantry Division) in the attack of the Hurtgen Forest, Germany, 19-21 November 1944, p. 13

34. Moore, The Operations of Company C, 8th Infantry (4th Infantry Division) in the attack of the Hurtgen Forest, Germany, 19-21 November 1944, p. 14-15

35. Moore, The Operations of Company C, 8th Infantry (4th Infantry Division) in the attack of the Hurtgen Forest, Germany, 19-21 November 1944, p. 15

36. Moore, The Operations of Company C, 8th Infantry (4th Infantry Division) in the attack of the Hurtgen Forest, Germany, 19-21 November 1944, p. 17

37. Moore, The Operations of Company C, 8th Infantry (4th Infantry Division) in the attack of the Hurtgen Forest, Germany, 19-21 November 1944, p. 17-18

38. Moore, The Operations of Company C, 8th Infantry (4th Infantry Division) in the attack of the Hurtgen Forest, Germany, 19-21 November 1944, p. 18

39. Moore, The Operations of Company C, 8th Infantry (4th Infantry Division) in the attack of the Hurtgen Forest, Germany, 19-21 November 1944, p. 19

40. Moore, The Operations of Company C, 8th Infantry (4th Infantry Division) in the attack of the Hurtgen Forest, Germany, 19-21 November 1944, p. 19

41. Moore, The Operations of Company C, 8th Infantry (4th Infantry Division) in the attack of the Hurtgen Forest, Germany, 19-21 November 1944, p. 19-20

42. Moore, The Operations of Company C, 8th Infantry (4th Infantry Division) in the attack of the Hurtgen Forest, Germany, 19-21 November 1944, p. 20

43. Moore, The Operations of Company C, 8th Infantry (4th Infantry Division) in the attack of the Hurtgen Forest, Germany, 19-21 November 1944, p. 20-21

44. Moore, The Operations of Company C, 8th Infantry (4th Infantry Division) in the attack of the Hurtgen Forest, Germany, 19-21 November 1944, p. 21

45. Moore, The Operations of Company C, 8th Infantry (4th Infantry Division) in the attack of the Hurtgen Forest, Germany, 19-21 November 1944, p. 21-23

46. Moore, The Operations of Company C, 8th Infantry (4th Infantry Division) in the attack of the Hurtgen Forest, Germany, 19-21 November 1944, p. 24

47. Moore, The Operations of Company C, 8th Infantry (4th Infantry Division) in the attack of the Hurtgen Forest, Germany, 19-21 November 1944, p. 24-25

48. Moore, The Operations of Company C, 8th Infantry (4th Infantry Division) in the attack of the Hurtgen Forest, Germany, 19-21 November 1944, p. 25

49. Moore, The Operations of Company C, 8th Infantry (4th Infantry Division) in the attack of the Hurtgen Forest, Germany, 19-21 November 1944, p. 25-26

50. Moore, The Operations of Company C, 8th Infantry (4th Infantry Division) in the attack of the Hurtgen Forest, Germany, 19-21 November 1944, p. 26-27

51. Moore, The Operations of Company C, 8th Infantry (4th Infantry Division) in the attack of the Hurtgen Forest, Germany, 19-21 November 1944, p. 27

52. Moore, The Operations of Company C, 8th Infantry (4th Infantry Division) in the attack of the Hurtgen Forest, Germany, 19-21 November 1944, p. 27

53. Moore, The Operations of Company C, 8th Infantry (4th Infantry Division) in the attack of the Hurtgen Forest, Germany, 19-21 November 1944, p. 27-28

54. Moore, The Operations of Company C, 8th Infantry (4th Infantry Division) in the attack of the Hurtgen Forest, Germany, 19-21 November 1944, p. 28

55. Moore, The Operations of Company C, 8th Infantry (4th Infantry Division) in the attack of the Hurtgen Forest, Germany, 19-21 November 1944, p. 28-29

56. Moore, The Operations of Company C, 8th Infantry (4th Infantry Division) in the attack of the Hurtgen Forest, Germany, 19-21 November 1944, p. 29

57. Moore, The Operations of Company C, 8th Infantry (4th Infantry Division) in the attack of the Hurtgen Forest, Germany, 19-21 November 1944, p. 29-30

58. Moore, The Operations of Company C, 8th Infantry (4th Infantry Division) in the attack of the Hurtgen Forest, Germany, 19-21 November 1944, p. 31

59. Moore, The Operations of Company C, 8th Infantry (4th Infantry Division) in the attack of the Hurtgen Forest, Germany, 19-21 November 1944, p. 31

60. Moore, The Operations of Company C, 8th Infantry (4th Infantry Division) in the attack of the Hurtgen Forest, Germany, 19-21 November 1944, p. 32

61. Moore, The Operations of Company C, 8th Infantry (4th Infantry Division) in the attack of the Hurtgen Forest, Germany, 19-21 November 1944, p. 32

62. Moore, The Operations of Company C, 8th Infantry (4th Infantry Division) in the attack of the Hurtgen Forest, Germany, 19-21 November 1944, p. 32-22

63. Moore, The Operations of Company C, 8th Infantry (4th Infantry Division) in the attack of the Hurtgen Forest, Germany, 19-21 November 1944, p. 33

64. Moore, The Operations of Company C, 8th Infantry (4th Infantry Division) in the attack of the Hurtgen Forest, Germany, 19-21 November 1944, p. 33

65. Moore, The Operations of Company C, 8th Infantry (4th Infantry Division) in the attack of the Hurtgen Forest, Germany, 19-21 November 1944, p. 34

66. Moore, The Operations of Company C, 8th Infantry (4th Infantry Division) in the attack of the Hurtgen Forest, Germany, 19-21 November 1944, p. 34-35

67. Moore, The Operations of Company C, 8th Infantry (4th Infantry Division) in the attack of the Hurtgen Forest, Germany, 19-21 November 1944, p. 35

68. Moore, The Operations of Company C, 8th Infantry (4th Infantry Division) in the attack of the Hurtgen Forest, Germany, 19-21 November 1944, p. 35-36

69. Moore, The Operations of Company C, 8th Infantry (4th Infantry Division) in the attack of the Hurtgen Forest, Germany, 19-21 November 1944, p. 36-37

70. Moore, The Operations of Company C, 8th Infantry (4th Infantry Division) in the attack of the Hurtgen Forest, Germany, 19-21 November 1944, p. 37

71. Moore, The Operations of Company C, 8th Infantry (4th Infantry Division) in the attack of the Hurtgen Forest, Germany, 19-21 November 1944, p. 37

72. Moore, The Operations of Company C, 8th Infantry (4th Infantry Division) in the attack of the Hurtgen Forest, Germany, 19-21 November 1944, p. 37

73. Moore, The Operations of Company C, 8th Infantry (4th Infantry Division) in the attack of the Hurtgen Forest, Germany, 19-21 November 1944, p. 38

74. Moore, The Operations of Company C, 8th Infantry (4th Infantry Division) in the attack of the Hurtgen Forest, Germany, 19-21 November 1944, p. 38

75. Moore, The Operations of Company C, 8th Infantry (4th Infantry Division) in the attack of the Hurtgen Forest, Germany, 19-21 November 1944, p. 38-39

76. Moore, The Operations of Company C, 8th Infantry (4th Infantry Division) in the attack of the Hurtgen Forest, Germany, 19-21 November 1944, p. 39

77. Moore, The Operations of Company C, 8th Infantry (4th Infantry Division) in the attack of the Hurtgen Forest, Germany, 19-21 November 1944, p. 39

78. Moore, The Operations of Company C, 8th Infantry (4th Infantry Division) in the attack of the Hurtgen Forest, Germany, 19-21 November 1944, p. 39-40

79. Moore, The Operations of Company C, 8th Infantry (4th Infantry Division) in the attack of the Hurtgen Forest, Germany, 19-21 November 1944, p. 40

80. Bill Loy, From tree to tree – One man's account of the battle of the Hurtgen Forest, High school project video

81. Action Against Enemy Reports After/After Action Reports, period 1 November 1944 – 30 November 1944, p. 9

82. Action Against Enemy Reports After/After Action Reports, period 1 November 1944 – 30 November 1944, p. 10

83. Bill Loy, From tree to tree – One man's account of the battle of the Hurtgen Forest, High school project video

84. Action Against Enemy Reports After/After Action Reports, period 1 November 1944 – 30 November 1944, p. 10

85. Ausland, Letters Home: A War Memoir

86. . Action Against Enemy Reports After/After Action Reports, period 1 November 1944 – 30 November 1944, p. 10-11

87. Action Against Enemy Reports After/After Action Reports, period 1 November 1944 – 30 November 1944, p. 11

88. Action Against Enemy Reports After/After Action Reports, period 1 November 1944 – 30 November 1944, p. 11

89. Bill Loy, From tree to tree – One man's account of the battle of the Hurtgen Forest, High school project video

90. Action Against Enemy Reports After/After Action Reports, period 1 November 1944 – 30 November 1944, p. 11-12

91. Action Against Enemy Reports After/After Action Reports, period 1 November 1944 – 30 November 1944, p. 12

92. Action Against Enemy Reports After/After Action Reports, period 1 November 1944 – 30 November 1944, p. 12-13

93. Action Against Enemy, Reports After/After Action Reports, period 1 December 1944 – 31 December 1944, p. 3

94. Action Against Enemy, Reports After/After Action Reports, period 1 December 1944 – 31 December 1944, p. 3

95. Recommendation for Award of the Distinguished Service Cross, Private Pedro Cano, 30 December 1944

96. Distinguished Service Cross citation, Sergeant Francisco G. Delgado

97. Recommendation for Award of the Distinguished Service Cross, Private Pedro Cano, 30 December 1944

98. Action Against Enemy, Reports After/After Action Reports, period 1 December 1944 – 31 December 1944, p. 3

99. Action Against Enemy, Reports After/After Action Reports, period 1 December 1944 – 31 December 1944, p. 3-4

100. Recommendation for Award of the Distinguished Service Cross, Private Pedro Cano, 30 December 1944

101. Action Against Enemy, Reports After/After Action Reports, period 1 December 1944 – 31 December 1944, p. 4

102. Distinguished Service Cross citation, Sergeant Francisco G. Delgado

103. Recommendation for Award of the Distinguished Service Cross, Private Pedro Cano, 30 December 1944

104. Fabian, The Untellable Story

105. Action Against Enemy, Reports After/After Action Reports, period 1 December 1944 – 31 December 1944, p. 4

106. Action Against Enemy, Reports After/After Action Reports, period 1 December 1944 – 31 December 1944, p. 4

107. Action Against Enemy, Reports After/After Action Reports, period 1 December 1944 – 31 December 1944, p. 4-5

108. Bill Loy, From tree to tree – One man's account of the battle of the Hurtgen Forest, High school project video

109. Action Against Enemy, Reports After/After Action Reports, period 1 December 1944 – 31 December 1944, p. 5

110. Action Against Enemy, Reports After/After Action Reports, period 1 December 1944 – 31 December 1944, p. 5-6

111. Action Against Enemy, Reports After/After Action Reports, period 1 December 1944 – 31 December 1944, p. 6

112. Action Against Enemy, Reports After/After Action Reports, period 1 December 1944 – 31 December 1944, p. 6

113. Action Against Enemy, Reports After/After Action Reports, period 1 December 1944 – 31 December 1944, p. 6-7

114. Action Against Enemy, Reports After/After Action Reports, period 1 December 1944 – 31 December 1944, p. 7

115. Action Against Enemy, Reports After/After Action Reports, period 1 December 1944 – 31 December 1944, p. 7-8
116. Action Against Enemy, Reports After/After Action Reports, period 1 December 1944 – 31 December 1944, p. 8
117. Action Against Enemy, Reports After/After Action Reports, period 1 December 1944 – 31 December 1944, p. 8
118. Action Against Enemy, Reports After/After Action Reports, period 1 December 1944 – 31 December 1944, p. 8
119. Action Against Enemy, Reports After/After Action Reports, period 1 December 1944 – 31 December 1944, p. 8
120. Action Against Enemy, Reports After/After Action Reports, period 1 December 1944 – 31 December 1944, p. 8-9
121. Action Against Enemy, Reports After/After Action Reports, period 1 December 1944 – 31 December 1944, p. 9
122. Action Against Enemy, Reports After/After Action Reports, period 1 December 1944 – 31 December 1944, p. 9
123. Recommendation for Award of the Distinguished Service Cross, Private Pedro Cano, 30 December 1944
124. Edinburg Valley Review, March 29, 1946
125. Edinburg Valley Review, March 29, 1946
126. Edinburg Valley Review, March 29, 1946
127. Edinburg Valley Review, March 29, 1946
128. Edinburg Valley Review, March 29, 1946
129. Edinburg Valley Review, April 20, 1946
130. Edinburg Valley Review, April 20, 1946
131. Edinburg Valley Review, April 20, 1946
132. Edinburg Valley Review, April 20, 1946
133. List of foreign-born Medal of Honor recipients http://en.wikipedia.org/wiki/List_of_foreign_born_Medal_of_Honor_recipients
134. Edinburg Valley Review, April 20, 1946
135. Edinburg Valley Review, April 20, 1946
136. Edinburg Valley Review, April 20, 1946
137. Edinburg Valley Review, April 20, 1946
138. Edinburg Valley Review, April 20, 1946
139. Edinburg Valley Review, April 20, 1946
140. Edinburg Valley Review, April 20, 1946
141. Edinburg Valley Review, April 20, 1946
142. Edinburg Valley Review, April 20, 1946
143. Edinburg Valley Review, April 20, 1946
144. Edinburg Valley Review, March 29, 1946
145. Edinburg Valley Review, March 29, 1946
146. Edinburg Valley Review, March 29, 1946
147. Edinburg Valley Review, March 29, 1946
148. Edinburg Valley Review, March 28, 1946
149. Edinburg Valley Review, April 1, 1946
150. Brownsville Herald, May 19, 1946
151. Edinburg Valley Review, April 1, 1946
152. Edinburg Valley Review, April 1, 1946
153. Edinburg Valley Review, April 1, 1946
154. Edinburg Valley Review, April 1, 1946
155. Edinburg Valley Review, April 2, 1946
156. Edinburg Valley Review, April 2, 1946
157. Edinburg Valley Review, April 4, 1946
158. Edinburg Valley Review, April 1, 1946
159. Edinburg Valley Review, April 1, 1946
160. Edinburg Valley Review, April 1, 1946

161. Edinburg Valley Review, April 5, 1946
162. Edinburg Valley Review, April 25, 1946
163. Edinburg Valley Review, April 25, 1946
164. Evening Valley Monitor, April 12, 1946
165. Evening Valley Monitor, April 12, 1946
166. Evening Valley Monitor, April 12, 1946
167. Evening Valley Review, April 20, 1946
168. Evening Valley Review, April 20, 1946
169. Evening Valley Review, April 20, 1946
170. Evening Valley Monitor, April 25, 1946
171. Evening Valley Monitor, April 25, 1946
172. Evening Valley Monitor, April 25, 1946
173. Edinburg Valley Review, April 26, 1946
174. Valley Evening Monitor, April 25, 1946
175. Edinburg Valley Review, April 20, 1946
176. Recommendation for Award of the Distinguished Service Cross, Private Pedro Cano, 30 December 1944
177. Valley Evening Monitor, April 25, 1946
178. Edinburg Valley Review, April 26, 1946
179. Edinburg Valley Review, April 26, 1946
180. Edinburg Valley Review, April 20, 1946
181. The Austin American, April 26, 1946
182. Evening Valley Monitor, April 25, 1946
183. Evening Valley Monitor, April 25, 1946
184. Evening Valley Monitor, April 25, 1946
185. Evening Valley Monitor, April 25, 1946
186. The daily Review, June 25, 1952
187. Hidalgo County News, July 3, 1952
188. Hidalgo County News, July 3, 1952
189. Interview with Aaron Pena, May 23, 2018
190. Progress Times, April 2, 2010
191. Progress Times, April 2, 2010
192. Governor Rick Perry, Texas Legislative Medal of Honor ceremony May 18, 2010
193. Sen. Juan Hinojosa, HCR 5, 81st Regular Session
194. 2002 National Defense Authorization Act
195. March 19, 2014, CSA's Valor 24 Hall of Heroes Induction ceremony, Chief of Staff of the Army, Gen. Ray Odierno
196. March 19, 2014, CSA's Valor 24 Hall of Heroes Induction ceremony, Secretary of Defense, Chuck Hagel

www.ingramcontent.com/pod-product-compliance
Lightning Source LLC
Chambersburg PA
CBHW071334130626
46556CB00004B/1900